W9-CMB-600

DISEASES & DISORDERS

Mental Retardation

Melissa Abramovitz

LUCENT BOOKS

An imprint of Thomson Gale, a part of The Thomson Corporation

THOMSON

™

GALE

Detroit • New York • San Francisco • New Haven, Conn. • Waterville, Maine • London

For more information, contact
Lucent Books
27500 Drake Rd.
Farmington Hills, MI 48331-3535
Or you can visit our Internet site at http://www.gale.com

LIBRARY OF CONGRESS CATALOGING-IN-PUBLICATION DATA

Abramovitz, Melissa, 1954–
   Mental retardation / by Melissa Abramovitz.
      p. cm. — (Diseases and disorders)
   Includes bibliographical references and index.
   ISBN-13: 978-1-59018-412-7 (hardcover)
   1. Mental retardation--Juvenile literature. I. Title.
   RC570.A27 2007
   616.85'88—dc22   2007006798

ISBN-10: 1-59018-412-2
Printed in the United States of America

Table of Contents

"The Most Difficult Puzzles Ever Devised"

Charles Best, one of the pioneers in the search for a cure for diabetes, once explained what it is about medical research that intrigued him so. "It's not just the gratification of knowing one is helping people," he confided, "although that probably is a more heroic and selfless motivation. Those feelings may enter in, but truly, what I find best is the feeling of going toe to toe with nature, of trying to solve the most difficult puzzles ever devised. The answers are there somewhere, those keys that will solve the puzzle and make the patient well. But how will those keys be found?"

Since the dawn of civilization, nothing has so puzzled people— and often frightened them, as well—as the onset of illness in a body or mind that had seemed healthy before. A seizure, the inability of a heart to pump, the sudden deterioration of muscle tone in a small child—being unable to reverse such conditions or even to understand why they occur was unspeakably frustrating to healers. Even before there were names for such conditions, even before they were understood at all, each was a reminder of how complex the human body was, and how vulnerable.

While our grappling with understanding diseases has been frustrating at times, it has also provided some of humankind's most heroic accomplishments. Alexander Fleming's accidental discovery in 1928 of a mold that could be turned into penicillin has resulted in the saving of untold millions of lives. The isolation of the enzyme insulin has reversed what was once a death sentence for anyone with diabetes. There have been great strides in combating conditions for which there is not yet a cure, too. Medicines can help AIDS patients live longer, diagnostic tools such as mammography and ultrasounds can help doctors find tumors while they are treatable, and laser surgery techniques have made the most intricate, minute operations routine.

This "toe-to-toe" competition with diseases and disorders is even more remarkable when seen in a historical continuum. An astonishing amount of progress has been made in a very short time. Just two hundred years ago, the existence of germs as a cause of some diseases was unknown. In fact, it was less than 150 years ago that a British surgeon named Joseph Lister had difficulty persuading his fellow doctors that washing their hands before delivering a baby might increase the chances of a healthy delivery (especially if they had just attended to a diseased patient)!

Each book in Lucent's Diseases and Disorders series explores a disease or disorder and the knowledge that has been accumulated (or discarded) by doctors through the years. Each book also examines the tools used for pinpointing a diagnosis, as well as the various means that are used to treat or cure a disease. Finally, new ideas are presented—techniques or medicines that may be on the horizon.

Frustration and disappointment are still part of medicine, for not every disease or condition can be cured or prevented. But the limitations of knowledge are being pushed outward constantly; the "most difficult puzzles ever devised" are finding challengers every day.

What's in a Name?

Mental retardation is a condition that involves lower-than-normal levels of intellectual functioning and adaptive behaviors. People with mental retardation have been called *idiots*, *imbeciles*, *retards*, *feebleminded*, and similar terms that hurt their feelings and relegate them to an outsider status in society. This is because of stereotypes that others assign to people with this condition. As Troy, a mentally retarded teen, relates: "Not too long ago, people with disabilities could not go to school with other kids. They had to go to 'special schools.' They could not have real friends. They call people like me 'retard.' That breaks my heart."[1]

People with mental retardation still face ridicule and feedback from others that says they are somehow less than human. But with a change in the language used to describe the disorder has come positive changes in the way mentally retarded people are perceived. Nowadays, the official name for this condition is *mental retardation*, and along with this less stigmatizing name has come more acceptance and inclusion of mentally retarded people.

Access and Acceptance

By law, mentally retarded children are guaranteed access to public schools and inclusion in regular classrooms as much as possible. Also by legal decree, mentally retarded children and adults must be given access to public places such as restaurants, theaters, and stores, and employers cannot deny employment to mentally retarded people who can fulfill the requirements of a given job. Yet many mentally retarded people and advocates for them point out that even with antidiscrimination laws in place, there is still a long way to go until people who suffer from mental retardation are fully accepted and included in society. Most people with mental retardation are unemployed. Parents of mentally retarded children still have to fight to have their child included in regular classrooms. Mentally retarded parents regularly have their children taken away from them even when they are capable of raising them independently.

Controversy over Terminology

Part of the problem, many advocates and self-advocates maintain, is that even the term *mental retardation* has a stigmatizing effect and promotes misconceptions about the capabilities and potential of those with mental retardation. This negative image is a result of the fact that many people view all who have mental retardation as being incapable of learning and social interactions. Advocates and self-advocates have argued that terms like *learning disability* or *developmental disability* are less offensive and have lobbied for usage of these alternative labels. Others have promoted the use of terms for medical disorders such as *Down syndrome* or *fragile X syndrome*, which are specific syndromes that cause the condition of mental retardation and some physical abnormalities in some individuals.

But many people who are mentally retarded do not suffer from these syndromes or other clearly defined medical disorders, and for some the cause of their condition is unknown, so the use of such terms would not be applicable to all. That is why *mental retardation* is still the most commonly used descriptor in the United States. In the British Commonwealth and in materials written by the International Society for the Scientific Study of Intellectual Disabilities, the term *intellectual disability* is most often used. In other places throughout the world, terms like *limitation, impairment, disability,* and *handicap* are used.

A boy with Down syndrome (center) hangs out with his nondisabled friends.

Although many family members, health-care professionals, and advocates would prefer that the medical profession and the public use terms other than *mental retardation* in the United States, changing the language would not be convenient or easy. As pointed out in a 2002 article on Social Security Online:

> Most people who "have" the condition that for about 50 years we have termed "mental retardation," and some of their allies, will never be satisfied with any designating term for them whatsoever, even though some designation is necessary in many situations in order for the state, condition, or class at issue to be appropriately communicated about [and the individuals can be offered appropriate medical treatment, legal protection, and special assistance]. If one is trying to find a term . . . that will finally satisfy those to whom it will be applied, one may as well give up this quest as futile, because there is no such term, and there never will be.[2]

It would also be difficult to change the term *mental retardation* because it is used as a diagnosis for eligibility for certain federal and state government programs, including special education, job-training programs, social security, and medical-fee assistance programs. Were alternative terms to be used, the laws and guidelines governing these programs would have to be changed. Several states have elected to use other terms for determining eligibility for special education in that state, and this has caused confusion in administering and tracking these programs throughout the United States. For example, some states refer to mentally retarded individuals as "developmentally disabled" even though the legal definition of developmental disability encompasses a far wider range of mental and physical impairments than does mental retardation. They do this in an attempt to attach less offensive language to the condition. But this results in confusion in labeling the patient and in confirming eligibility for certain programs. The use of alternative terms has also caused confusion in legal matters such as death penalty prosecutions and legal guardianship issues relating to adults with mental retardation.

The Goal of Advocacy

The controversy over the term *mental retardation* will most likely continue as advocates and self-advocates seek to replace it with a modern, less offensive label. Although the American Association on Mental Retardation (AAMR) did vote to change its name to the American Association on Intellectual and Developmental Disabilities in June 2006, it is not known how this will impact preferred terminology. But for the time being, the term *mental retardation* is still the most widely used in the United States and will probably remain as such even while alternatives are being promoted. No matter what the condition is called, however, the common goal for advocates and self-advocates is to have mentally retarded people enjoy acceptance and inclusion in all aspects of society and in this manner to enjoy more fulfilling, productive lives. As stated in the position statement of The Arc of the United States, an organization that promotes the rights and welfare of those with mental retardation:

Many of our constituents have not had the opportunity or the support to control choices and decisions about important aspects of their lives. Instead, they are often overprotected and involuntarily segregated. Many of these people have not had opportunities to learn the skills and have the experiences that would enable them to take more personal control and make choices. The lack of such learning opportunities and experiences has denied people with these disabilities the right to become participating, valued, and respected members of their communities.[3]

Only when they are granted such rights, says The Arc, will mentally retarded people be able to give back fully to the communities in which they live.

CHAPTER ONE

What Is Mental Retardation?

Mental retardation has affected people since the beginning of human history. The first historical references to the condition were found in Egyptian papyri dated around 1552 B.C. In ancient Egypt, mental retardation was considered to be a disease caused by brain damage. Although it was recognized as a disease, it was not measured or clearly defined.

It was not until the 1900s that the disorder became clearly defined and diagnosed as a condition involving a lack of normal intelligence. Intelligence refers to general mental capacity— the ability to reason, plan, understand, and learn. Intelligence quotient (IQ) tests were used to determine individuals' mental capacity and ability to adapt to their environment. (An IQ of 100 is considered average.) Those who scored below 75 were diagnosed as having mental retardation.

In addition to IQ scores lower than 75, experts also developed a classification system that identified different degrees of retardation in order to describe more clearly the severity of the disability. A 1910 classification of the mentally retarded by the American Association on Mental Deficiency identified three levels of retardation: an *idiot* was considered to be someone whose mental development stopped at the level of a two-year-old, an *imbecile* was an individual whose level of functioning at maturity was equivalent to that of a two-to-seven-year-old,

11

and a *moron* was someone whose mental development stopped at the level of a seven-to-twelve-year-old. These terms were later determined to be offensive and were replaced by other labels such as *mildly, moderately, severely,* and *profoundly retarded.*

Modern Definitions of Mental Retardation

Modern definitions of mental retardation emphasize that mental retardation is not a specific disease. Instead, it is a condition that results from a variety of medical disorders. All people with mental retardation share the traits of having below-average intelligence and less-than-normal mental capabilities to adapt to their environment. In order to qualify as mental retardation, these traits must appear before age eighteen.

There are two main definitions of mental retardation accepted in the United States and one used throughout the world. The first one was developed in 1992 by the American Association on Mental Retardation (which, as of June 2006, changed its name to the American Association on Intellectual and Developmental Disabilities), and is generally the most accepted definition in the United States. The AAMR definition specifies that persons with an IQ of less than 70 to 75 are mentally retarded. Furthermore, it defines mental retardation as

> substantial limitations in present functioning. It is characterized by significantly subaverage intellectual functioning, existing concurrently with related limitations in two or more of the following applicable adaptive skill areas: communication, self-care, home living, social skills, community use, self direction, health and safety, functional academics, leisure and work. Mental retardation manifests before age 18.[4]

The second widely accepted definition in the United States was developed by the American Psychiatric Association and appears in the fourth edition of the *Diagnostic and Statistical Manual of Mental Disorders* (DSM-IV). This definition is nearly identical to the AAMR definition in terms of specifying that an IQ score of 70 or below and certain impairments in

David Wechsler

Dr. David Wechsler developed some of the most commonly administered intelligence tests used today. Wechsler was born in 1896 in Lespedi, Romania. He studied at City College of New York and at Columbia University, where he obtained his PhD in psychology in 1925. He held a variety of positions as a clinical psychologist, the most noteworthy being chief psychologist at the Bellevue Psychiatric Hospital in New York from 1932 to 1967. While in this position he developed a battery of intelligence tests known as the Wechsler-Bellevue Intelligence Scale.

Wechsler viewed intelligence as a combination of the ability to think rationally and to deal with one's environment; this notion remains prevalent in modern thought about what constitutes intelligence. Over the years he developed several measurement scales to test intelligence in different age groups, including the Wechsler Intelligence Scale for Children, the Wechsler Adult Intelligence Scale, and the Wechsler Preschool and Primary Scale of Intelligence. Wechsler died in 1981 in New York City.

adaptive functioning be present. But the DSM-IV criteria also include *levels* of retardation, which are important to know in determining the capabilities and potential of the individual being diagnosed. The level of *mild* retardation applies to people with an IQ of between 50 and 70; *moderate* retardation covers those with an IQ of 35 to 50; *severe* is 25 to 35; and *profound* is below 20.

The third definition of mental retardation is based on the *International Statistical Classification of Diseases and Related Health Problems*, tenth revision (ICD-10), criteria recognized throughout much of the world. It defines mental retardation as "a condition of arrested or incomplete development of the mind characterized by impaired developmental skills that contribute to the overall level of intelligence."[5] The

ICD-10 also refers to four levels of retardation. *Mild* retardation encompasses an IQ level of 50 to 69 and is diagnosed in individuals who acquire language and self-care skills later than normal but who speak and take care of themselves reasonably well. They generally can read, write, and work when given simple tasks. *Moderate* retardation applies to people with an IQ of between 35 and 49 who can master limited language skills and are impaired in taking care of themselves. Moderately retarded people can do simple work but need a supervised, structured setting. *Severely* mentally retarded people have an IQ of 20 to 34 and have little or no language skills and limited motor skills. *Profound* mental retardation is diagnosed in an individual with an IQ below 20 who cannot learn, move around, or provide for his or her own basic needs.

The ICD-10 definition also refers to mental age in assessing the degree of retardation. Someone who is mildly retarded is said to have a mental age of nine to less than twelve; moderate retardation corresponds to a mental age of six to less than nine; severe retardation has a mental age of three to less than six; and profound retardation has a mental age of less than three.

How Is Mental Retardation Diagnosed?

Diagnosing and classifying mental retardation involves a mental-health professional administering one or more standardized intelligence tests and at least one standardized adaptive-skills test. The doctor also observes behavior, emotions, and physical attributes and interviews family members for further information on intelligence and behavior. Sometimes mental retardation can be diagnosed in an infant, especially if there are also physical abnormalities present, which is often the case for those who suffer from syndromes such as Down syndrome or cri du chat syndrome. Other times it is not until a baby shows signs of taking longer to learn to speak, walk, and care for personal needs such as eating and toileting that mental retardation is diagnosed. In cases where retardation is mild, parents and professionals may not suspect the condition until a child has started school and has difficulty learning.

Examples of tests used to diagnose mental retardation throughout the world include the Bayley Scales of Infant Development, a test used to assess the development of infants and very young children. This test is appropriate for children aged two months to three-and-a-half years old. It is composed of three scales (measurements): the mental scale, the motor scale, and the behavior rating scale. The mental scale measures short-term memory, recognition memory, attention, imitation, vocal

Babies who take longer to learn to speak or walk may have some form of mental retardation.

skills, early language, and similar skills. The motor scale measures motor skills such as grasping objects and walking. The behavior rating scale assesses the child's behavior and emotions during the evaluation. Lower-than-normal scores in any or all categories can indicate mental retardation.

The Wechsler Intelligence Scale for Children is an example of an assessment used for children aged six through sixteen years. It contains thirteen subtests and includes measurements of vocabulary, arithmetic, comprehension, picture completion, picture arrangement, object assembly, coding, and other areas. The test gives three separate IQ readings consisting of verbal IQ, performance-scale IQ, and full-scale IQ. When administered by a trained examiner, this test gives a reliable comprehensive IQ score that can be used to assess the presence and severity of mental retardation.

For measuring adaptive behavior, a necessary part of the definition and diagnosis of mental retardation, experts assess how well an individual functions and meets personal and social demands. The most common measurement scale used is the Vineland Adaptive Behavior scales. This measures communication, daily-living skills, socialization, and motor skills in people from birth through age nineteen. Someone familiar with the individual's behavior, such as a parent, answers a series of questions in each area, and the scores from each domain are combined to yield an adaptive behavior composite score.

Who Is Affected by Mental Retardation?

Based on these or similar tests, mental-health experts diagnose and classify mental retardation. According to the AAMR, at the present time such diagnosis has led to the knowledge that in the United States there are approximately 2.5 million people, or 1 to 3 percent of the population, affected by varying degrees of retardation. The condition is found in people of all racial, ethnic, social, and economic backgrounds, though it does affect more males than females and more blacks than whites.

In general, the life expectancy for all people with mental retardation is shorter than normal, in part because of physical abnormalities and in part because of reduced access to health

A girl taking the Wechsler IQ test.

care. The life expectancy of individuals with mental retardation is shortest for those with severe or profound retardation, who tend to have a variety of physical problems along with diminished mental capacity. Mental retardation is also associated with an increased risk for other brain disorders, such as seizures and mental illness, though these disorders do not always go along with mental retardation.

Doctors emphasize that mental retardation is different from mental illness. Mental illnesses are severe disturbances in mood, behavior, and thought processes that may exist in retarded as well as nonretarded individuals. Examples of mental illnesses are schizophrenia and bipolar disorder. They have little to do with intelligence and are often related to imbalances in brain chemistry.

Types of Mental Retardation

Although all forms of mental retardation share the characteristics of intellectual impairment and difficulties with adaptive behaviors, there are still many specific types of retardation that vary in severity and underlying cause. For this reason, doctors who diagnose the disorder are faced with a wide range of symptoms and degree of impairment, often making diagnosis difficult.

The most familiar form of retardation is Down syndrome, described in 1866 by the English physician John Langdon Haydon Down. Down syndrome is also a cause of mental retardation. It affects about 350,000 people in the United States. It is the most familiar type of mental retardation because it affects so many people and because it involves easily recognizable physical abnormalities. People with the syndrome exhibit moderate to severe mental retardation and rarely have an IQ over 50. They also typically have physical abnormalities such as slanted eyes with small skin folds at the inner corner of the eyes (a characteristic known as mongolism), a flat nose, short stature, short neck, small, flattened skull, and small mouth with protruding tongue. Individuals with Down syndrome also commonly have a single crease across the palm of their hands, reduced muscle tone, heart defects, and incomplete sexual development.

Not all people with the syndrome exhibit all the symptoms, and sometimes not enough symptoms are present to make a diagnosis at birth. Once a child grows out of infancy the diagnosis is easier to make, especially because the defects in intelligence and the abnormal physical growth become more apparent. Even so, there is a wide range of mental abilities and developmental progress in people with Down syndrome. For example, some people with the syndrome can graduate from high school, while others are not capable of learning beyond a fifth- or sixth-grade level.

Because of advancements in modern medicine, the life expectancy for a person with Down syndrome has increased from twelve years to nearly forty. The medical problems that typically affect people with Down syndrome are congenital (inborn) heart disease, gastrointestinal abnormalities, congenital cataracts in the eyes, nearsightedness, hearing loss, low thyroid hormone production, and nystagmus (abnormal side-to-side eye movements).

Children with Down syndrome tend to show developmental problems in addition to impaired mental abilities. They do not

John Langdon Haydon Down

John Langdon Haydon Down was born in 1828 in Torpoint, Cornwall, England. He developed an interest in science at an early age but left school at age thirteen to assist his father, who was a pharmacist. At age eighteen he moved to London and supported himself as an assistant to a surgeon. In 1847 he began working as a research assistant in organic chemistry and went on to assist Michael Faraday, one of the greatest scientists of all time, in his experiments with gases.

At age twenty-five Down entered medical school in the London Hospital and graduated with honors in 1858. He then became a resident physician and, later on, medical superintendent at the Earlswood Asylum for Idiots in Surrey. He also set up a practice at the London Hospital and divided his time between this practice and the Earlswood institution.

Down published a great deal of work on mental health and disease and advocated for training children with mental disabilities. He set up the first institution of its kind for this purpose in 1869. In 1887 he published *Mental Affections of Childhood and Youth*, a description of the condition that now bears his name—Down syndrome. Down died in 1896 in Hampton Wick.

usually learn to walk until they are fifteen to thirty-six months old, whereas most children begin walking at eleven to fourteen months. Children with Down syndrome are, however, calm and cooperative, unlike many children with other forms of mental retardation. Once Down syndrome children reach adolescence, many experience emotional and behavioral difficulties that seem typically to go along with the syndrome, often becoming defiant and depressed. As they age into their thirties, many people with Down syndrome begin to show a deterioration in language skills, memory, problem-solving ability, and self-care skills. Doctors believe this is due to problems in the brain similar to those seen in patients with Alzheimer's disease. Alzheimer's is generally seen in people over age sixty, but the same brain changes occur much earlier in people with Down syndrome.

These young people have Down syndrome.

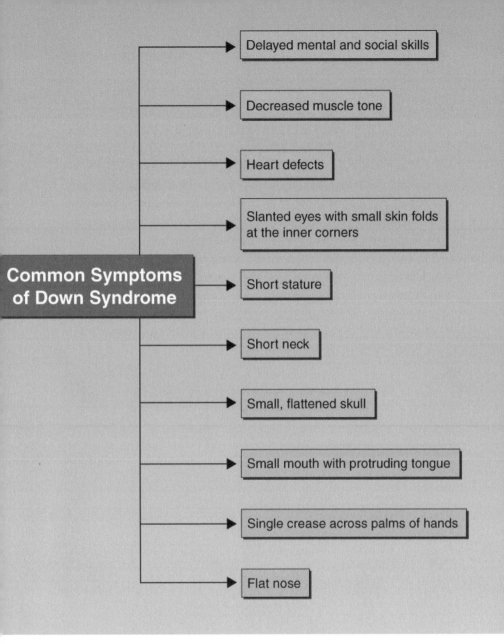

Common Symptoms of Down Syndrome

- Delayed mental and social skills
- Decreased muscle tone
- Heart defects
- Slanted eyes with small skin folds at the inner corners
- Short stature
- Short neck
- Small, flattened skull
- Small mouth with protruding tongue
- Single crease across palms of hands
- Flat nose

Fragile X Syndrome

Another well-known form of mental retardation is fragile X syndrome. Symptoms of this syndrome vary widely between individuals. Some people with the disorder have mild defects in intelligence, while others have retardation that is severe. The intelligence of people with fragile X syndrome declines during puberty, no matter how high or low it is during childhood.

Besides mental retardation, people with fragile X syndrome also often have physical abnormalities such as short stature, a large head with a narrow face and long ears, a prominent forehead, long, soft hands, double-jointed fingers, and large testicles in adolescent boys. While most of these abnormalities are present at birth, even then the syndrome is often not diagnosed right away. The first clues that parents may have of its presence is an inability of the baby to cuddle, fussiness, or inability to learn a routine. Other clues are delayed walking or talking.

Cassie, a baby with fragile X syndrome, started out seemingly normal, but soon her parents began to suspect that something was wrong. According to her mother, Fran:

A young man who has fragile X syndrome stands outside of his West Virginia apartment complex.

Cassie was an easy baby—for about 2 months! Then she became inconsolable. In the church nursery, helpers stopped cuddling or even picking her up because even that didn't help. She had constant ear infections and missed all her milestones [like sitting up, walking, and talking]. Our doctor continued to reassure us that she was just a late bloomer but a friend in the know suggested that we test Cassie's attention and language. At age 2, she tested at a nine-month level! The results allowed us to get the help and support we so desperately needed.[6]

Rett Syndrome

Rett syndrome, another condition that causes mental retardation, was first described in 1966 by the Austrian pediatrician Andreas Rett. It is found only in females. There are four stages of Rett syndrome. Stage one is called early onset and generally begins between six and eighteen months of age. Physical symptoms may include loss of muscle tone, reduced eye contact, and delays in development of motor skills such as sitting or crawling. This stage lasts anywhere from a few months to more than a year.

Stage two is the rapid destructive phase. It appears between the ages of one and four and is characterized by the loss of hand skills and speech. Hand-wringing or hand-washing repetitive motions appear during this stage. The child's head slows in growth and becomes noticeably smaller than normal. Breathing irregularities such as fast breathing begin. The child becomes irritable and may have trouble sleeping.

Stage three is the plateau or pseudo-stationary stage. It begins between ages two and ten and may last for years. Stage three includes motor problems, seizures, and some improvements in behavior with less irritability and crying and more alertness and communication. Many patients remain in this stage for much of their lives.

In stage four, the late motor deterioration stage, walking becomes difficult if not impossible. Muscles become stiff, and the spine begins to curve abnormally. Mental skills generally remain about the same during this phase and can range from mild to profound retardation.

This boy has autism, a developmental disability that is often confused with Rett syndrome.

Rett syndrome is often difficult to diagnose and distinguish from other syndromes that involve mental retardation. It is also frequently confused with autism or cerebral palsy because of similarities in symptoms. Autism is a developmental disability that affects social interaction and communication skills. Cerebral palsy is a neurological condition that affects body movement and muscle coordination. Many suspected sufferers have to go to a special clinic and receive multiple tests before they are correctly diagnosed with Rett syndrome rather than one of these other conditions.

Angelman Syndrome

Another condition that produces mental retardation is Angelman syndrome, first described in 1965 by the English physician Harry Angelman, who explains his discovery:

It was purely by chance that [in 1964] three handicapped children were admitted at various times to my children's ward in England. They had a variety of disabilities and although at first sight they seemed to be suffering from different conditions I felt that there was a common cause for their illness. The diagnosis was purely a clinical one because in spite of technical investigations which today are more refined I was unable to establish scientific proof that the three children all had the same handicap. In view of this I hesitated to write about them in the medical journals. However, when on holiday in Italy I happened to see an oil painting in the Castelvecchio Museum in Verona called . . . a Boy with a Puppet. The boy's laughing face and the fact that my patients exhibited jerky movements gave me the idea of writing an article about the three children with a title of Puppet Children. It was not a name that pleased all parents but it served as a means of combining the three little patients into a single group. Later the name was changed to Angelman syndrome. This article was published in 1965 and after some initial interest lay almost forgotten until the early eighties.[7]

Besides the characteristic jerky movements, Angelman syndrome also involves severe mental retardation, a small head with a wide, smiling mouth, thin upper lip, protruding tongue, and pointed chin. Many affected people have fair hair, blue eyes, crossed eyes, seizures, and lack of speech. Sometimes Angelman syndrome is still referred to as the "happy puppet" syndrome because of the jerky gait, smiling mouth, and frequent, inappropriate laughter.

Angelman syndrome is generally not diagnosed at birth or in infancy because the disabilities seen are fairly nonspecific at this time. Usually it is diagnosed between the ages of three and seven when the characteristic symptoms become more evident. This syndrome is thought to affect one in fifteen thousand to one in twenty thousand people.

Cri du Chat Syndrome

Cri du chat (French for "cry of the cat") syndrome is another disorder accompanied by moderate to severe mental retardation.

It is called cri du chat because affected infants have a catlike cry due to an abnormal voice box. This catlike cry disappears with age. Other characteristics of cri du chat syndrome include a small head, low-set ears, slanted eyes, small jaws, a wide brow with an abnormally wide space between the eyes and eyebrows, partial webbing of the fingers and toes, and a single line in the palm of the hand. The characteristic catlike cry is the symptom that generally leads to a diagnosis of cri du chat syndrome in infancy. This syndrome is quite rare—it occurs in about one in twenty-five thousand to one in fifty thousand births. Many affected children do not live to adulthood, though some do.

People with cri du chat syndrome may achieve milestones such as walking and talking later in life than a normal child would. Mindy, for example, was never expected to sit up, walk, or talk, but she started walking at age two and learned to speak in three- to six-word sentences. She was unable to read or write but learned to swim with a flotation device. She was easily startled and frightened of many things, exhibited obsessive behaviors, and had frequent temper tantrums. But she is an example of one of the higher-functioning individuals with cri du chat.

Prader-Willi Syndrome

Prader-Willi syndrome is another condition that involves mental retardation. It was first described by Doctors Prader, Labhart, and Willi in a report that detailed an unusual pattern of symptoms including decreased activity in the fetus, poor muscle tone, and feeding problems in infancy. These feeding problems were due to weak muscles which prevented the baby from bottle feeding. The feeding difficulties were replaced by an uncontrollable hunger and compulsive eating phase that emerged between two and three years old and lasted for the remainder of the individual's life. The uncontrollable hunger led to obesity, and most people with Prader-Willi syndrome require constant supervision to keep them from eating constantly. Many families have to put locks on food cupboards and refrigerators to keep the person from compulsive eating.

Prader-Willi syndrome also includes a variety of other symptoms. Affected persons display an IQ of between 20 and 85 (severe retardation to low normal intelligence, depending on the individual; some with the syndrome do not have mental retardation). They frequently exhibit angry, defiant behavior and compulsive actions that may include skin picking, hair pulling, tantrums, hand washing, and counting. Physically, people with Prader-Willi syndrome have short stature, soft and easily broken bones, soft teeth, thick saliva, small hands and feet, and underdeveloped sex organs. This syndrome affects approximately one in every twelve to fifteen thousand people.

Cornelia de Lange Syndrome

Cornelia de Lange syndrome is a disorder that always involves mental retardation. It was originally described in 1933 by the Dutch pediatrician Cornelia de Lange, who noticed that two children with similar physical features and mental deficiencies were admitted within weeks of each other to a children's hospital where she worked. The first child, aged seventeen months, had pneumonia, and her first year of life included feeding difficulties. She was very small for her age and had a very small head. The second patient, aged six months, had similar medical problems and closely resembled the first little girl. De Lange was unable to find similar patients described in the medical literature, and the syndrome now bears her name.

The syndrome affects about one in ten thousand people. It involves numerous physical abnormalities as well as mild to profound mental retardation. Most sufferers have severe retardation. Symptoms are usually evident at birth, and diagnosis can usually be made at birth or shortly thereafter.

Infants with the syndrome have problems with swallowing and vomiting, often resulting in liquid being sucked into the lungs and causing pneumonia. Babies and small children with the disorder do not grow at a normal rate. They have prominent eyebrows that join in the middle of the forehead; long, curled eyelashes; and a small upturned nose. The mouth is typically turned down with thin lips. The limbs are abnormally small, with the fingers malformed and the second and third toes webbed. Children with Cornelia de Lange syndrome tend to have heavy body hair and hearing impairment, which results in a lack of speech. Internally, they often have inborn heart disease and intestinal abnormalities. Besides mental retardation, children with Cornelia de Lange have behavioral abnormalities such as disliking being held and exhibiting compulsive behaviors like teeth grinding and finger biting. They are also likely to injure themselves deliberately.

Other Types of Mental Retardation

The specific syndromes associated with mental retardation do not affect all persons who are mentally retarded. Some of those with mental retardation only have the condition without other characteristics that may accompany it as seen in the various syndromes. Others have mental and physical deficiencies that do not fit any known disorder. That is why diagnosing the different forms of mental retardation can be challenging and why understanding the causes of mental retardation can be important in making a diagnosis.

CHAPTER TWO

What Causes Mental Retardation?

Mental retardation can be caused by a variety of factors that affect the structure and function of the brain. There have been several hundred causes identified. In about a third of mentally retarded people, though, the cause is unknown.

Because brain development begins early in fetal development and continues after birth through adolescence, the brains of fetuses, babies, and children are especially vulnerable to injury or malfunction from various internal or external environmental factors. The precise effects depend on exactly when during development the damage occurs.

According to the American Association on Mental Retardation:

> It is likely that a large percentage of cases of MR [mental retardation] have more than one causal factor. At least our current understanding suggests that multiple factors play a role in many cases. It is important, therefore, to have a dynamic view of the individual in the context of biological, physical, environmental, and psychosocial factors. A vulnerable individual may develop intellectual function and adaptive skills better or worse, depending on the nature of the environment in which he/she is situated.[8]

Genetic and Chromosomal Abnormalities

Researchers have found that the most common known cause of mental retardation is genetic and chromosomal abnormalities. These abnormalities cause the majority of cases of severe mental retardation. Genes are the part of a deoxyribonucleic acid (DNA) molecule that pass hereditary information from parents to their children. They reside on wormlike bodies called chromosomes in the center, or nucleus, of each cell. The sequence of genes on each chromosome provides the cell containing the chromosomes with a set of instructions on how to grow and operate. A baby is born with two copies of this instruction set—one from each parent.

Humans have forty-six chromosomes in each cell. Twenty-three come from the mother and the other twenty-three from the father. The genes on each chromosome also come in pairs, with one copy of every gene from the mother and one from the father.

When a gene or chromosome is damaged, the resulting change is called a mutation. The damage that produces a mutation can involve an entire chromosome, one or more genes, or one or more of the chemicals that make up DNA. A DNA molecule is composed of two strands of chemical compounds known as nucleotides, which include the chemical bases ade-

Chromosomes, as seen under a microscope. Genetic and chromosomal abnormalities are the most common cause of mental retardation.

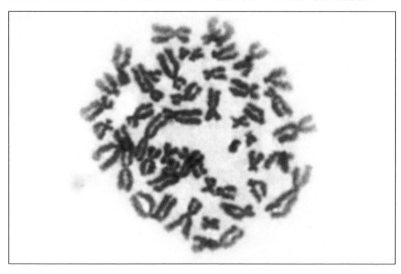

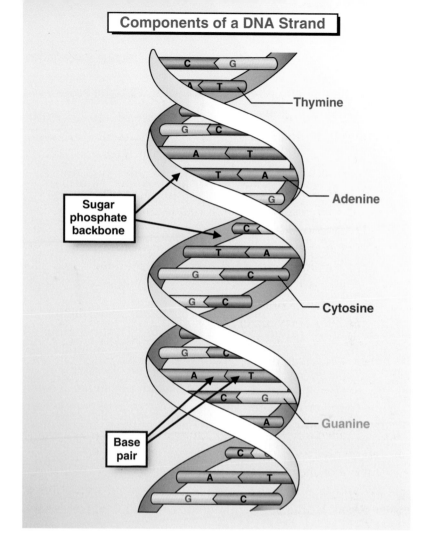

Components of a DNA Strand

Thymine

Sugar phosphate backbone

Adenine

Cytosine

Guanine

Base pair

nine, thymine, guanine, and cytosine. These strands are twisted together so that adenine is always paired with thymine and guanine with cytosine. The exact sequence of nucleotides determines the instructions encoded in a particular gene. Damage or absence of even one nucleotide is sometimes enough to totally disrupt the instructions associated with the gene.

Mutated genetic material can be passed to a child if it happens to be part of the set of chromosomes and genes transmitted from either the mother or father. Sometimes mutations are not transmitted from the parents but result from later damage to the genes and chromosomes during a person's development. Either way, the altered genetic instructions may cause various malfunctions that produce certain diseases or disorders. There are more than five hundred mutations known to be associated with mental retardation.

Chromosome Abnormalities and Down Syndrome

Some genetic disorders may have chromosome abnormalities that cause mental retardation. These disorders can be caused by too many or too few chromosomes or by structural defects in the chromosomes. In most cases the abnormalities are not inherited directly from the parents. Instead, they develop due to spontaneous damage to the chromosome at conception or during fetal growth.

Mental retardation caused by chromosome abnormalities is most commonly found in Down syndrome. Of the estimated 2.5 million people in the United States who have mental retardation, about 350,000, or 14 percent, have the disorder as a result of Down syndrome. In 1959 the French physician Jerome Lejeune found an extra chromosome in the cells of people with the disorder. Later studies determined that the extra chromosome was a copy of number 21; thus Down syndrome is often referred to as trisomy 21 because affected persons have three

Jerome Lejeune

Jerome Lejeune was a French physician who discovered the cause of Down syndrome. He was born in 1926 in the Parisian suburb of Montrouge and later became a doctor and a research scientist with the French National Scientific Research Organization. In 1958 he was examining under a microscope the chromosomes of a child with Down syndrome and discovered that there was an extra twenty-first chromosome. This was the first time that a link had been established between a chromosome abnormality and mental retardation. Lejeune and his colleagues went on to discover a host of other chromosome defects, and many experts consider him to be one of the foremost scientists who paved the way for the science of modern genetics.

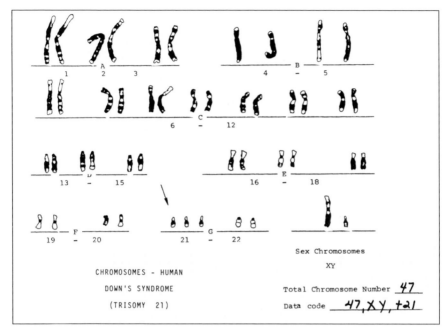

A chromosome map of a person with Down syndrome. An arrow points to the twenty-first pair of chromosomes, which show the presence of a third chromosome, the cause of Down syndrome.

copies of chromosome 21. The extra copy of this chromosome means that someone with Down syndrome has forty-seven instead of forty-six chromosomes in each cell. This extra chromosome consists of extra genes that cause mental retardation and other characteristic symptoms of the syndrome.

The extra chromosome generally comes from the mother rather than from the father. This occurs most often in women who have babies when they are over thirty years old. The risk of this happening is one in one hundred births for women aged thirty-two and older and one in thirty births for women aged forty-five and older.

Although scientists understand that the extra chromosome 21 causes Down syndrome, no one is sure what triggers this mutation. Some doctors believe that hormones, X rays, viral infections, immune system problems, or a genetic predisposition may be the underlying cause, but none of these factors has been proven to be responsible.

Fragile X Syndrome

The second most common genetic cause of mental retardation after Down syndrome is fragile X syndrome. Unlike Down syndrome, fragile X syndrome is inherited, resulting from a gene mutation in the FMR1 gene on the X chromosome. The X chro-

Illustration of an X chromosome featuring the anomaly associated with fragile X syndrome. The anomaly consists of a slender thread at the bottom that links to the rest of the chromosome. This thread is easily broken.

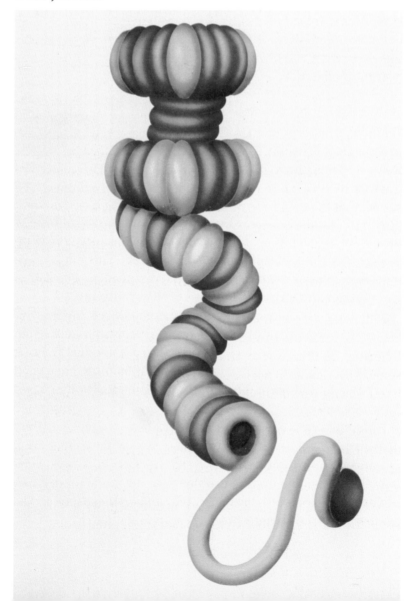

mosome is a sex chromosome; girls have two X chromosomes, while boys have one X chromosome and one Y chromosome. The disorder is called fragile X syndrome because it renders the X chromosome fragile and subject to breakage at the site of the mutation.

The gene mutation shuts down production of the FMR1 protein. This protein is essential for normal brain function, and loss of it affects development, behavior, and physical features. The effects on males are generally more severe than those on females. Most males with fragile X syndrome have mild to severe mental retardation. One-third of females with the disorder have mental retardation ranging from mild to severe, one-third have only learning disabilities, and one-third have normal intellectual development.

Missing Genes and Mutations

Cri du chat syndrome is another syndrome caused by a genetic abnormality. It results from a missing piece of chromosome 5. Researchers believe the symptoms of the disorder come from the loss of several genes on this chromosome. Studies have shown that the larger the number of missing genes on the chromosome, the more severe the mental retardation and other symptoms such as small head, catlike cry, and inability to walk or talk. The mutation that causes cri du chat syndrome is not inherited. It develops randomly during the formation of egg or sperm cells prior to conception.

Rett syndrome is another syndrome that causes mental retardation. It results from a random mutation rather than being inherited, in this case in the MECP2 gene on the X chromosome. This mutation does not allow DNA to be correctly translated during cell division. If this mutation occurs in a male fetus, it is lethal prior to birth because there is no normal X chromosome to make up for the damaged X chromosome. Females can live with the MECP2 mutation because they have another X chromosome that can be normal and provide for some functions essential to life.

Angelman syndrome is caused by a mutation on chromosome 15 that is inherited from the mother. A similar mutation on chromosome 15 inherited from the father causes Prader-Willi syndrome. These two syndromes are different because maternal and paternal copies of the affected gene play different roles in development. The genetic problem that results in Angelman syndrome is a missing section on chromosome 15 that contains the gene UBE3A. Deletion of this gene causes the lack of a protein called ubiquitin that is necessary for normal brain function.

With Prader-Willi syndrome, the disorder is caused by the absence of one or more contiguous genes on chromosome 15 from the father. This genetic defect leads to a flaw in the hypothalamus of the brain, the part that determines hunger and fullness. That is why sufferers of Prader-Willi syndrome exhibit compulsive eating. The genetic defect also affects other parts of the brain that control learning and behavior.

Cornelia de Lange syndrome, another cause of mental retardation, results from a defect in the gene NIPBL located on chromosome 5. This gene is involved in the early stages of embryonic development and contains the information needed to make a protein that helps switch on a number of other genes. This protein is called delangin. Mutations in NIPBL lead to an abnormal version of delangin, and this in turn disrupts the normal development of intelligence, as well as contributing to other features that are abnormal in Cornelia de Lange syndrome.

Gene Mutations and Metabolic Defects

Some genetic mutations cause metabolic defects that are in turn linked to mental retardation. Metabolic defects result in the inability to use certain chemicals in the body. According to the authors of *Understanding Mental Retardation:*

> Mutations that block a metabolic pathway represent the greatest number of known causes of retardation. The abnormal effects result from a buildup of metabolic products before the block or the lack of a necessary product behind it. Left undiagnosed and untreated, these inborn conditions generally lead to mental retardation. Early diagnosis, treatment, and regular evaluation are keys to re-

ducing the effects of such disorders in affected newborns and infants.[9]

The most common defect of metabolism that causes mental retardation is phenylketonuria (PKU), which was first described in 1934 by Dr. Asbjorn Folling and which affects one in twelve thousand to fifteen thousand babies born in the United States. PKU can be caused by over forty different mutations on chromosomes 12, 4, or 11. It results in an infant being unable to metabolize the amino acid phenylalanine. This in turn leads to phenylalanine and its derivative, phenylpyruvic acid, building up to toxic levels that produce brain damage.

All babies born in the United States are routinely screened for PKU with a blood test. If the defect is detected, treatment

Asbjorn Folling

Dr. Asbjorn Folling discovered PKU in Norway in 1934. A woman brought her two severely mentally retarded children to him because she noticed they had a musty odor coming from them. Folling did not find anything significant when he examined the children, but then he took urine samples and tested the urine with ferric chloride, a substance used to detect chemicals called ketones in the urine of diabetics. Normal urine remains brownish when ferric chloride is added, and urine with ketones turns purple or burgundy in the presence of this chemical. To Folling's surprise, the two children's urine turned dark green when ferric chloride was added. Neither he nor any other doctors had seen this happen before.

After much research and testing, Folling found that the reason for this chemical reaction was the presence of phenylpyruvic acid in the urine. This chemical is excreted when there are high levels of it in the blood. Folling tested several hundred people with mental retardation and found more who had this abnormal chemical. He suggested that an inherited problem that prevented the use of phenylalanine caused the condition.

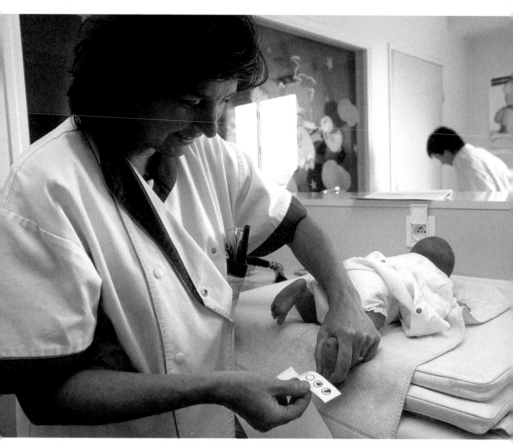

This newborn is being tested for PKU. All newborns in the United States are screened for PKU.

can be started before brain damage occurs. Doctors find that treatment begun before age three months can prevent mental retardation. However, if a baby does not inherit PKU but the mother has PKU that is not controlled by diet, the baby is still at risk for mental retardation. When this happens, the mother's high levels of phenylalanine in the blood can cause mental retardation in the newborn. These effects cannot be treated in the baby because he or she does not actually have PKU.

Prenatal Environmental Causes

Besides genetic causes of mental retardation, there are also environmental conditions in the uterus that can affect a fetus before it is born. "The environment in the uterus has a pro-found impact, both physically and intellectually, on the development of the child,"[10] say the authors of *Understanding Mental Retardation*. One harmful prenatal influence can be in-sufficient blood flow to the fetus, which can result in inade-quate oxygen and nutrients and in a failure to remove waste products from the uterine environment. If this occurs when the brain is developing, mental retardation may result.

Certain environmental conditions in the uterus can lead to mental retardation.

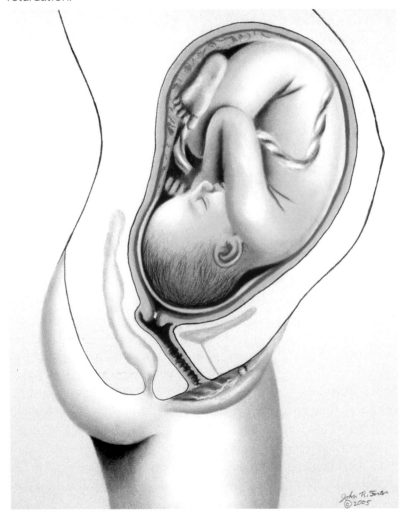

Another harmful influence is toxic chemicals inhaled or consumed by the mother. This may be from exposure to lead, pesticides, or other toxic chemicals in the environment. Lead is one of the most well-known substances that are toxic to the brain. It once was used in house paint, but this was banned in the United States in 1978. However, lead is still used in some household products, toys, and calcium supplements that the mother may have contact with.

Other well-known toxic substances that can harm a fetus are flame retardants found in furniture, clothing, and electronic products; tobacco smoke; polychlorinated biphenyls (PCBs) found in some meat, fish, and dairy products; and mercury, found in some fish. Toluene, a toxin found in glue and gasoline, can also be toxic to a developing fetus if the mother inhales these substances during pregnancy.

Other Toxic Influences

A particularly dramatic example of the effects of the toxin mercury took place in Japan in the 1950s, when mercury was discharged into rivers and coastal waters. Fish contaminated with high levels of mercury were eaten by residents of Minamata and Niigata. Many people became ill with severe neurological diseases, and several hundred died. Pregnant women who ingested the fish gave birth to babies with severe developmental disabilities, including mental retardation. The outcome became known as Congenital Minamata disease. Since this outbreak, experts have warned pregnant women not to eat too much fish because of the dangers of mercury poisoning.

Other potential toxic influences can come from the mother taking any of many types of prescription and nonprescription drugs which can cause mental retardation and numerous physical abnormalities in the developing fetus. The most common such maternal source of birth defects is drinking alcohol while pregnant. This causes fetal alcohol syndrome (FAS). FAS is responsible for 10 to 20 percent of cases of mental retardation with IQs in the 50 to 80 range. Alcohol causes severe retardation when taken during certain critical periods of brain development. When a pregnant mother drinks alcohol, the drug

This boy has fetal alcohol syndrome.

passes through the placenta and enters the fetus through the umbilical cord. Then it affects the size, shape, and function of cells in the baby's brain and other organs.

Injuries to the mother that result in blood loss or damage to the uterus can also lead to mental retardation in the developing fetus. So can poor health in the mother, including conditions like severe thyroid deficiency, poorly controlled diabetes, AIDS, syphilis, toxoplasmosis (which comes from undercooked meat or from cats, horses, or birds), and Rh factor blood incompatibilities between mother and fetus. Rh blood disease occurs when a woman with Rh negative blood has a baby with Rh positive blood. The mother makes antibodies to the Rh positive blood contacted during childbirth, and these antibodies may then attack the red blood cells of an Rh positive baby during a subsequent pregnancy. This attack can cause jaundice, a liver disorder, in the baby. Severe jaundice can result in mental retardation.

If a woman develops a viral infection, especially early in the pregnancy, this can also produce mental retardation in the baby. One of the most common viruses to cause this effect is rubella, also known as German measles. This is generally a mild infection in children and adults. But when it strikes a pregnant woman during the first month of pregnancy, the fetus has a 50 percent chance of developing severe birth defects, including mental retardation. Infection with the rubella virus during subsequent months of pregnancy can also be serious.

Malnourishment and vitamin deficiencies in the mother can also cause mental retardation in the fetus, particularly during the first six months of pregnancy. One of the most common vitamin deficiencies linked to mental retardation is the B vitamin folate. If folic acid supplements are taken during the first month of pregnancy, this can help prevent damage to the nervous system. That is why many doctors recommend that women routinely take folic acid supplements during their childbearing years.

Events During or After Childbirth

Events that occur during or shortly after childbirth can also be critical in causing mental retardation. A baby that is born prematurely and has low birth weight is at higher-than-normal risk for physical and intellectual abnormalities. Another event that can cause mental retardation is if the baby receives inadequate or no oxygen while it is being born. This can happen if the umbilical cord gets wrapped around the baby's neck or if the child is born in a breech position (feet first). The delivery itself can also cause mental retardation if forceps are used to guide the head through the birth canal and undue pressure resulting in brain damage is applied. During birth, if a baby catches the sexually transmitted disease herpes simplex type 2 from an infected mother and the baby goes on to develop herpes simplex encephalitis (a severe infection of the brain), this can also result in brain damage and mental retardation

Events During Childhood

During childhood, certain injuries and illnesses can lead to brain damage and mental retardation. When these factors affect an individual below age eighteen and result in diminished intellectual functioning, by definition that person has mental retardation. Some experts estimate that about 15 percent of children with mild mental retardation get the condition from

Bonnie Armstrong, president of the Shaken Baby Alliance, holds a demonstration doll used to educate people about the dangers of shaken baby syndrome.

A little girl sits next to a wall with peeling paint. One cause of lead poisoning is ingesting chips from old house paint. Lead poisoning during childhood can lead to mental retardation.

head trauma. This trauma can come from child abuse, falls, bicycle accidents, car accidents, shaken baby syndrome (where a baby or young child is vigorously shaken by the arms, legs, chest, or shoulders), and near-drowning where the brain is deprived of oxygen.

One particularly gruesome case involving mental retardation from severe trauma was the case of Luis Mata, a mentally retarded man who was executed in 1996 for the crimes that he committed. Mata suffered organic brain damage from multiple medical traumas and had an I.Q. tested variously between 63 and 70. Mata's alcoholic father beat all of his sixteen children, but he picked primarily on Luis, subjecting him to constant physical abuse—kicking him, punching him, and beating him with electrical cords. When Luis Mata was six, he fell off a truck, badly fracturing his skull, but his family was too poor to obtain medical treatment for him. This and other medical traumas may have contributed to his neurological deficits.[11]

In turn, authorities believed that Mata's mental retardation played a role in the crimes he committed, rendering him unable to understand right from wrong. Because of many such cases where mentally retarded defendants were determined not to be able to distinguish right and wrong, people with mental retardation today are protected from the death penalty.

Another cause of mental retardation during childhood is lead poisoning. Lead is known as a neurotoxin, or a substance that is toxic to the nervous system. Lead poisoning can result from inhaling fumes from leaded paints or from ingesting chips from old house paint. Federal regulations now require that house paints contain no lead, but older buildings may still have paint with lead in it. Drinking water from lead pipes and repeatedly inhaling leaded gasoline can also cause lead poisoning.

Other Neurotoxic Chemicals

There are many other chemicals besides lead that are known to harm children's brains. These chemicals are all said to be neurotoxic. According to experts from many research centers, these chemicals are everywhere—in schools, homes, industries, toys, and food products. Many are not regulated by the government, and organizations like the AAMR have called for more research and oversight into their use to prevent vulnerable individuals from exposure.

An example of a commonly found harmful toxin is bisphenol A, a component in many plastic products like baby bottles and food containers. Bisphenol A is an industrial chemical used primarily to make polycarbonate plastic and epoxy resins. Polycarbonate is clear, lightweight, and shatter resistant. It is used in reusable food and drink containers, in electronics, and in making bullet-resistant glass. Epoxy resins are used as linings in metal cans to keep food and beverages from spoiling. They are also used in electrical equipment, adhesives, and protective coatings. When released from such compounds, bisphenol A has been shown to cause chromosomal defects associated with mental retardation. It can be released from plastics if a child chews on the products or if the product is washed in a bleach solution.

Certain childhood illnesses can lead to mental retardation if they involve meningitis or encephalitis, inflammations of the lining of the brain and of the brain itself, respectively. These illnesses include Reyes syndrome, whooping cough, chicken pox, measles, and Hib disease (Haemophilus influenzae type b, a bacteria that causes bacterial meningitis). Doctors point out that these diseases do not always cause mental retardation; instead retardation occurs when a certain level of brain damage is produced. Brain damage is more likely if these illnesses remain untreated.

A Variety of Causes

Given the wide range of potential causes of mental retardation, the question arises as to whether any of these factors can be prevented. While some factors cannot be prevented by any means, there are others that can be avoided through a variety of measures. And when mental retardation cannot be prevented, there are things that can be done to provide remediation and treatment for many who are affected.

CHAPTER THREE

Prevention, Remediation, and Treatment

Although there is no cure for mental retardation if someone has it, there are certain things that can be done to prevent, remediate, and treat the condition. Some cases of mental retardation can be prevented by screening for or eliminating the causes. For example, screening for PKU using a blood test in newborns and providing appropriate dietary treatment if PKU is found helps prevent several hundred babies from getting mental retardation each year in the United States. Women with PKU can also follow a special diet when they are pregnant to prevent mental retardation in the baby. When pregnant women with PKU do not follow a strict diet, infants born to them have a 93 percent chance of having mental retardation.

Screening newborns for low thyroid hormone and giving them appropriate doses of this hormone as needed helps prevent about one thousand cases of mental retardation each year in the United States. The use of iodized salt also helps prevent low thyroid hormone and subsequent retardation. This is why iodine is added to salt as a preventive measure in many countries.

Another condition infants are commonly screened for is galactosemia. This is the lack of an enzyme necessary to digest

Infants with galactosemia cannot digest dairy products and may develop liver damage and mental retardation.

dairy products. If an infant with galactosemia is given milk, it often dies within a few days from liver failure. Those who survive after ingesting milk develop liver damage and mental retardation. By being screened for this disorder, a baby can then be given a nondairy formula and avoid death or mental retardation.

In combination with screening newborns for specific disorders, certain treatments can prevent the development of mental retardation. Kernicterus, for example, is a type of brain damage that results from a bad case of jaundice in a newborn. It can be prevented by using special lights or other therapies to treat the jaundice immediately. Jaundice is a condition where the liver makes too much of a yellow pigment called bilirubin. When too much bilirubin builds up in the body, the skin and whites of the eyes turn yellow. Mild jaundice is fairly common in newborns and usually goes away by itself. But when a baby has severe jaundice, the high levels of bilirubin can damage the brain and result in mental retardation.

Other disorders that cause mental retardation can be prevented through vaccination or other medications that affect the immune system. Giving anti–Rh immune globulin, a substance that keeps the mother's immune system from destroying the unborn baby's blood, helps to prevent Rh disease in newborns and over one thousand cases of mental retardation in the United States each year. Prevention of Hib disease by giving infants the Hib vaccine helps prevent over five thousand cases each year. Using the measles vaccine to prevent measles

A nurse prepares to inject the measles vaccine into the arm of a baby girl. The measles vaccine prevents over four thousand cases of mental retardation each year.

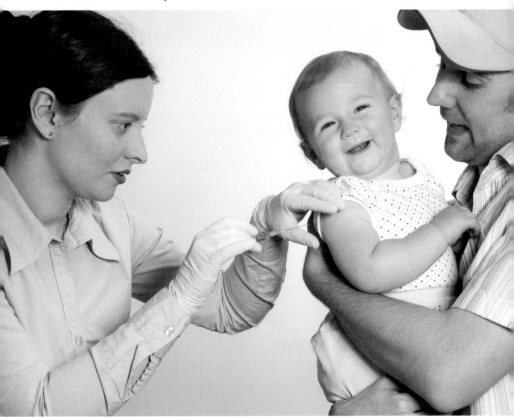

in infants and children prevents over four thousand cases of mental retardation yearly in the United States.

Other actions that society can take to reduce the risk of mental retardation include removing lead from the environment, encouraging the use of child safety car seats and bicycle helmets to prevent head trauma, and educating parents and caretakers about the dangers of shaken baby syndrome.

Pregnant mothers can help prevent the risk of mental retardation in their babies through good prenatal care and a balanced diet. Many expectant mothers take prenatal vitamins to make sure they are getting enough essential nutrients. Doctors recommend that pregnant women avoid alcohol, drugs, and smoking to help prevent mental retardation in the baby. Since

Hunter and Fetal Alcohol Syndrome

In the article "Meet Hunter," a boy with mental retardation caused by fetal alcohol syndrome (FAS) reveals why he hopes expectant mothers will help prevent FAS by not drinking alcohol:

I learned about FAS when I was twelve through a movie I was watching called "The Broken Cord." I saw this kid in this movie and I thought to myself, "Man, that kid is me." . . . Learning that I had FAS and what FAS was answered so many questions for me and explained why I had so many problems in school and why they called me "mentally retarded." I hated the term "mentally retarded" but having FAS wasn't as bad. I learned why I couldn't learn certain things and how I could learn best—why some days I can remember things and do certain things and some days it just doesn't click. . . . I just want mothers to know that because my mother drank, I am like I am, and that isn't so bad, but if you can stop one mother from drinking, that would be great too.

Quoted in The Arc, "Meet Hunter." www.thearc.org/fasproject/meethunter.htm.

some prescription and nonprescription medicines can be unsafe to use during pregnancy, women are advised to check with their doctors before taking any medication.

However, any amount of alcohol is not safe to ingest during pregnancy, and according to the surgeon general of the United States, Fetal Alcohol Syndrome is the number one preventable birth defect associated with mental retardation. Despite repeated warnings, some women continue to drink alcohol while pregnant. A report by the surgeon general advises:

1. A pregnant woman should not drink alcohol during pregnancy.

2. A pregnant woman who has already consumed alcohol during her pregnancy should stop in order to minimize further risk.

3. A woman who is considering becoming pregnant should abstain from alcohol.

4. Recognizing that nearly half of all births in the United States are unplanned, women of child-bearing age should consult their physician and take steps to reduce the possibility of prenatal alcohol exposure.[12]

One other method of preventing mental retardation is for a couple to receive genetic counseling before getting pregnant. If certain risk factors are present, the genetic counselor may advise the people not to have a baby. These risk factors may include having another child with mental retardation, the mother being thirty-five years old or older, and if the partners are blood relatives.

Remediation

When mental retardation cannot be prevented and a child is either born with the condition or acquires it later on, there are things that can be done to help many people who have mental retardation achieve maximum mental and physical potential. Special interventions designed to help with development are known as remediation. Examples of remediation might include special education, development plans, and drug and nutritional treatments.

A couple talks with their doctor. Couples with certain risk factors may seek out genetic counseling before getting pregnant.

The Early Roots of Special Education

Prior to the 1800s, experts and laypeople alike believed that individuals with mental retardation could not be helped by remediation. Mentally retarded people were typically kept at home or institutionalized. But then the French physician Jean-Marc-Gaspard Itard developed the first special education program to teach Victor, known as the Wild Boy of Aveyron, language, social skills, and living skills. Victor, who was mentally retarded, spent his early life in the wild with a pack of dogs in the woods of south central France. When he was found at age twelve, he had no language or social skills. Itard managed to teach the boy several useful behaviors. This surprised many mental-health experts and educators who believed that the mentally retarded could not be taught. Itard's success led to new efforts to educate the mentally retarded throughout Europe.

A former student of Itard's, Édouard Séguin, became one of the leaders in educating the mentally challenged children in France. Séguin developed a program known as the physiological method. This program emphasized teaching awareness of

Dr. Édouard Séguin

Édouard Séguin was born in Clamecy, France, in 1812. He was educated at the College of Auxerre and St. Louis, then went on to study medicine under Dr. Jean-Marc-Gaspard Itard. Séguin devoted himself to studying and trying to educate people with mental retardation, or "idiots," as they were then called. He opened the first school for idiots in 1839 and had remarkable success. His methods were copied elsewhere in the world. In 1848 he came to the United States and helped to open many schools for those with mental retardation; many experts view him as the single most important pioneer in education of this sort. In arguing for the importance of education for the mentally retarded, Séguin once noted that

> not one idiot in a thousand has been entirely refractory [immune] to treatment, not one in a hundred has not been made more happy and healthy; more than thirty percent have been taught to conform to social and moral law, and rendered capable of order, of good feeling, and of working like the third of a man; more than forty percent have become capable of the ordinary transactions of life under friendly control, of understanding moral and social abstractions, of working like two-thirds of a man.

Séguin died in 1880 in New York City.

Quoted in Virtual American Biographies, "Edouard Seguin." www.famousamericans. net/edouardseguin/.

the senses, coordination, self-care skills, and memory skills. When Séguin moved to the United States in 1848, he began efforts to educate the mentally retarded in America.

Another pioneer of special education in the United States was Samuel Gridley Howe, who began training children who were blind, deaf, and/or mentally retarded in 1838. Like children who were mentally retarded, those who were blind or had hearing or speech impairments were labeled as ineducable at this time. But under Howe's leadership, people who were mentally retarded, blind, or deaf had some success in learning. Howe helped to organize the opening of a special, experimental school for children with mental retardation in 1848, and in 1849 founded the Massachusetts School for Idiotic and Feeble-minded Youth.

Soon afterward the first legislation to establish special schools was enacted in New York. The New York State Asylum was opened in 1851 and later became known as the Syracuse State School. This school admitted only children who were considered educable, but even so did not make much progress in educating the youngsters so that they could function in the community. In fact, when they reached the age that the school directors determined that they should be sent home, many of the parents pressured the school to keep the children. This happened in many special schools that educated children with mental retardation, with the result

Samuel Gridley Howe.

that many turned into custodial institutions rather than just training schools.

Education in the Twentieth and Twenty-First Centuries

By the beginning of the twentieth century, many regular public and private schools throughout the United States began establishing special education classes for mildly mentally retarded children who were unable to keep up in a normal classroom. However, there were not enough teachers trained to educate these children, and many therefore ended up in institutions with more severely retarded individuals or just stayed at home and received no education.

Then in 1975 the U.S. Congress passed the Education for All Handicapped Children Act that guaranteed a public education for all retarded or otherwise handicapped children from birth through age twenty-one. The Individuals with Disabilities Education Act (IDEA), passed in 1997 and amended in 2004, further detailed criteria for defining disabilities and required each state to submit education plans for the disabled to the federal government. According to The Arc, an organization that promotes the rights and welfare of the mentally retarded, "The Individuals with Disabilities Education Act (IDEA) is a federal law mandating that all children with disabilities have available to them a free, appropriate public education that emphasizes special education and related services designed to meet their unique needs and prepare them for employment and independent living."[13]

This law includes a requirement that disabled students be educated with nondisabled students to the greatest extent possible. This is referred to as the least restrictive environment. However, in practice, many times the mentally retarded are isolated in a special classroom and do not interact with normal children. An article in *Insight*, a magazine that advocates for the mentally retarded, explains why this is so:

> The segregation of children and adults with disabilities in "special" settings . . . is an outcome of prejudicial perceptions and attitudes. And circular logic allows this prejudice

A non–special education girl works with a boy with Down syndrome. The Individuals with Disabilities Education Act requires that disabled students be educated with nondisabled students to the greatest extent possible.

to continue, in both theory and practice. In theory, when a person is in a segregated setting, it's assumed that's the "correct" place for him to be, so there he remains. Conversely, if people with disabilities are not visible in everyday environments, it's assumed they're unable to succeed in those environments. In practice, placing people in segregated, dependent settings often prevents them from learning how to be successful in typical environments. And again, conversely, their absence from typical environments (in school classrooms and elsewhere) prevents others from learning how to welcome them, how to "be" around them, how to provide the supports they may need, and so forth.[14]

Advocacy organizations are trying to integrate the mentally retarded as much as possible into society to alleviate these problems.

Individual Family Service Plans and Individualized Education Plans

Recognizing the importance of early intervention in helping mentally retarded children learn and function, IDEA also requires that each child receive an Individualized Education Plan (IEP) or an Individual Family Service Plan (IFSP) for infants and toddlers. The IFSP is designed to help disabled babies develop as fully as possible so as to prevent them from being institutionalized and to reduce later educational costs to society by minimizing the need for special education. Parents and families are taught by experts how to best care for a baby with mental retardation. The IFSP is written by health and education authorities in the community working together with the parents and is designed specifically for each child. A service coordinator is responsible for implementing the plan and for working with professionals who are part of the team that administers therapy and care. Each IFSP is reviewed every six months and updated annually or sooner if the child's needs change.

The IEP for school-aged children is similarly developed by education experts and the child's parents. It is based on test results formulated by psychologists, educators, and medical authorities. The IEP may include other appropriate types of therapy besides special education. It may include speech therapy, occupational therapy, and physical therapy as needed. Occupational therapy focuses on helping the child learn everyday self-care skills such as eating, dressing, and toileting. Physical therapy is administered by a physical therapist to try to correct or compensate for physical disabilities. These services may be received in public schools if an evaluation determines that the child is eligible, at home, or in an appropriate medical facility. A service coordinator helps find needed services and assists with an ongoing evaluation of special needs. An IEP is reviewed yearly by an assessment team to determine progress and future needs.

When a child is fourteen years old, IDEA requires that schools begin to help him or her with the transition from school to work as part of the IEP. This can include instruction in daily living skills, in vocational skills and interests, and in experiences to prepare the child for everyday needs such as shopping, managing finances, taking public transportation, and participating in recreational activities. Matthew, for example, learned to use public transportation at age fifteen so he will someday be able to get to and from a job. Matthew is interested in plants, so his IEP has been developed by him, his parents, and educators to teach him about jobs in forestry, landscaping, and grounds maintenance.

Even though public education is available to all mentally retarded children, some parents elect to teach their child at home. Patrick, for example, has cri du chat syndrome and is easily overwhelmed by too much sensory input, so his parents prefer to educate him at home with the help of several therapists. Patrick can identify shapes, colors, and pictures. He can say a few words but cannot color or draw because of delays in motor skill development. Various therapists help his parents work with him on motor skills and speech.

Drug and Nutritional Treatment

Special education is just one area that experts have promoted in an attempt to better the lives of the mentally retarded. Some doctors have recommended using drugs and nutrition as a method of making the mind and body function better. In the 1950s, for example, Dr. Henry Turkel came up with the idea of using drugs and nutrition to correct problems of metabolism in children with Down syndrome. Turkel believed that these metabolic problems led to a lack of oxygen in the body's cells, which in turn resulted in brain damage and mental retardation. He prescribed a combination of nutrients and drugs he believed would correct these problems. Included were vitamins, minerals, fatty acids, amino acids, digestive enzymes, thyroid hormone, antihistamines, and nasal decongestants. The combination of substances was known as the U-series.

Some parents claimed the U-series improved their children's language and reading skills along with their physical condition. However, scientific studies comparing patients given the U-series with those given a placebo (an inactive substance that looks like the real thing) showed no significant improvement in the physical or mental condition in the group receiving the U-series.

Despite the lack of scientific proof to support the notion that dietary supplements and drugs can better the condition of people with mental retardation, many doctors continue to prescribe such therapy, and some parents firmly believe the substances help their children. Patrick, for example, who has cri du chat syndrome, takes vitamin and mineral supplements, which his parents claim have enabled him to gain weight, concentrate, and speak better.

A mentally retarded girl using public transportation.

There is one type of mental retardation that has been proven to be helped by a special diet. This is retardation due to PKU. All newborns in the United States are screened for this disorder, and if a baby is found to have the condition, treatment consists of a diet low in phenylalanine. This involves giving the baby a special formula and later placing him or her on a diet that prohibits high-protein foods like meat, fish, eggs, poultry, dairy products, nuts, peanut butter, legumes, soy products, and anything containing the artificial sweetener aspartame. In the past, doctors believed that children could discontinue this diet by age five or six, but recent research has found that those who do not remain on the diet indefinitely have more developmental delays, learning disabilities, and other neurological problems.

Treatments for Specific Health Problems

With mental retardation other than that caused by PKU, there is not anything beyond special education that is proven to enhance the person's mental skills. However, there are various medical treatments for the health problems that often go along with various types of mental retardation. For example, those with Angelman syndrome often have seizures that require treatment with antiseizure medicines. Those with Rett syndrome often need medication for seizures and breathing difficulties. Braces may be needed to straighten the spine and to support the legs in some cases.

Babies and children with Down syndrome often need treatment for a variety of medical problems. Between 60 and 80 percent of children with Down syndrome have hearing loss, which requires ongoing evaluation and treatment with hearing aids. Between 40 and 50 percent of children with Down syndrome have inborn heart defects that must be treated with heart surgery. Many children also have gastrointestinal abnormalities like a blockage of the esophagus, small intestine, or anus that must be surgically corrected during infancy. Many have eye problems like cataracts, crossed eyes, nearsightedness, or farsightedness that must be corrected with surgery or glasses. A significant percentage of children with Down syndrome have low thyroid hormone, which must be given artificially.

Doctors point out that many physical problems experienced by the mentally retarded are not easy to diagnose and treat, because the individual is unable to communicate the nature of the disorder. For example, a person with Down syndrome who has hearing or visual difficulties may not know how to tell anyone about these difficulties. Experts recommend that caretakers be alert for changes in behavior that might indicate eye problems, such as rubbing the eyes, squinting, stumbling, or hesitancy on stairs, and schedule an eye exam if these behaviors occur. Similarly, behaviors such as turning up the television volume, speaking loudly, responding to questions inappropriately, or becoming confused when in a noisy situation may indicate hearing loss and should be addressed by scheduling an appointment with a hearing specialist.

Mental Retardation and Aging

As people with mental retardation age, they are subject to the same types of health problems as nonretarded persons, and they may not be able to communicate symptoms of such conditions as heart disease, cancer, diabetes, or osteoporosis. For this reason, doctors say that those with mental retardation should receive regular physical examinations to check for these types of health problems. This is especially true because the level of physical fitness is often poor for people who have mental retardation. Because of this they are more prone to diseases like heart disease, arthritis, type 2 diabetes, and respiratory diseases brought on by a sedentary lifestyle. According to The Arc: "The fitness levels of adults with mental retardation, in general, are terrible. So, as younger people with mental retardation age, their general lack of physical fitness on top of health problems that older people generally face increases the likelihood that many will have health problems beyond those of their nondisabled peers."[15] This means that, in addition to the special remediations that people with mental retardation require to compensate for their mental shortcomings, they also need a disproportionate amount of treatment for physical problems throughout much of their lives.

CHAPTER FOUR

Living with Mental Retardation

Living with mental retardation is challenging for many reasons. One reason is that people with the condition have experienced ostracism and discrimination since ancient times. In ancient Greek writings, references to mental retardation included documentation that newborns were examined by a council of elders. If a baby was found to be defective in any way, including mentally, it was destroyed. In ancient Rome people with physical or mental disabilities were often sold to be used for entertainment. During the Middle Ages many mentally retarded people were sold into slavery, though some were sent for special care in foundling homes.

At the beginning of the twelfth century, King Henry II of England supported legislation that named people with mental retardation as wards of the state, meaning that they were under the protection of the government. This was the first time such individuals were given any legal protection. But it was not until 1876, when the educator Édouard Séguin founded the Association of Medical Officers of American Institutions for Idiotic and Feeble Minded Persons to advocate for the mentally retarded that advocacy on a large scale began. This association later became the American Association on Mental Retardation (AAMR) and continues to be active in education and advocacy today.

But the mentally retarded still had a long way to go before overt discrimination was to be stifled. For instance, in 1905 the French physicians Alfred Binet and Théodore Simon developed objective tests for measuring intelligence that were supposed to be used to evaluate candidates for special education. These tests were translated and put into use in the United States by Henry Goddard, director of research at a training school for the mentally retarded in Vineland, New Jersey. Once widespread testing of children and adults began, however, the results were often used for purposes other than determining who needed special education. One such other purpose involved removing the

King Henry II of England supported legislation that placed people with mental retardation under the protection of the government.

Henry Goddard

Henry Goddard brought intelligence testing to the United
States when he translated the Binet-Simon intelligence test into
English in 1908. But he advocated using this test for more than
just determining who needed special education. Goddard
strongly believed that those who tested as "morons," "imbeciles,"
or "idiots" should be prevented from having children. He believed that mandatory sterilization would solve the problem, but
hesitated to promote this policy openly because he did not think
the American people would accept it. Instead he advocated that
the mentally retarded should be isolated in colonies.

By the late 1920s Goddard had changed his mind on many of
his views. He publicly announced that his concept of segregated
colonies for the mentally retarded had been wrong, and he as-
serted that feebleminded persons should be allowed to reproduce if they chose to do so. However, because of his earlier views
and actions, Goddard has always been associated with the eugenics philosophy.

mentally retarded from the mainstream of society. Finding that
many people in prison were mentally retarded as determined by
these tests, authorities began a movement to protect society
from such individuals. They institutionalized and sterilized the
mentally retarded so they could not reproduce and bear mentally retarded children. This was based on the erroneous as-
sumption that those with mental retardation would always
produce children who also had mental retardation.

This practice continued into the middle of the twentieth century. In a well-known U.S. Supreme Court case in 1927, for example, the Court upheld the right of the state of Virginia to
sterilize Carrie Buck, a retarded woman who had committed
no crime but whose mother and daughter were also retarded.
In explaining the Court's ruling, Justice Oliver Wendell Holmes
said: "It is better for all the world, if instead of waiting to exe-

cute degenerate offspring for crime or to let them starve for their imbecility society can prevent those who are manifestly unfit from continuing their kind. . . . Three generations of imbeciles are enough."[16]

In addition, many mentally deficient babies and children were euthanized, or killed, by doctors who believed they were doing what was best for all concerned. In Germany euthanasia was the official medical policy regarding mental retardation, beginning around 1920. In the United States it was never the official medical policy, but was still widely advocated and practiced.

Modern Rights

Today the mentally retarded are legally protected from euthanasia and forcible sterilization in most of the world. Those with mental retardation today have powerful advocacy organizations looking out for their rights, and many of them are involved in self-advocacy. They hold international, national, and statewide conferences to discuss and promote vital issues, assisted by nondisabled advisors.

One of the landmark pieces of legislation in the United States that guarantees these rights is the Americans with Disabilities Act of 1990. This law bans discrimination based on physical or mental disability and guarantees equal opportunities for such individuals in employment; public accommodations; transportation; national, state, and local government services; and telecommunications. This means that people with mental retardation cannot be denied access to jobs, transportation, or public places because of their disability. Like all other applicants, however, in order to be hired for a job they must meet the qualifications.

The law also states that special concessions have to be made to make public venues accessible to all. An example of how businesses can make a facility accessible to those with mental retardation would be if a bus driver gave special assistance to the person in getting off at the right bus stop. Another example would be posting pictures along with words to identify restrooms or departments in a store so that people who cannot read can still find things. Or, in a restaurant, a server can be trained to offer simple explanations of menu choices to a client who cannot read or understand the menu.

Advocacy groups for the mentally retarded regularly engage in monitoring businesses and government facilities to make sure they are in compliance with the Americans with Disabilities Act. Prior to passage of this legislation, mentally disabled individuals, especially those whose disabilities were physically obvious, were often discouraged from even appearing in public. It was not uncommon for restaurant owners, for example, to ask families with a Down syndrome member to leave so as not to make other customers uncomfortable. The act now protects them from this form of discrimination.

The Fight for Family Rights

Despite the laws that prohibit discrimination against people with mental retardation, there are still areas today where overt violations of these people's right to live a fairly normal life occur regularly. One of these areas is the right to be parents and raise children. According to The Arc:

> The rights to marry and raise children have long been recognized as fundamental under the Constitution of the United States. While these rights apply to parents who have intellectual disabilities, their parental rights have often been terminated solely upon the determination that a parent has an intellectual disability. There often has been no assessment of the parents' actual abilities or the likelihood that they could successfully parent with appropriate supports. The Arc's position statement on sexuality states that people with mental retardation and related developmental disabilities have the right to make decisions about having and raising children and to have access to the proper supports on an individual basis to assist them in raising their children within their own home.[17]

People with mental retardation, says The Arc, are often very capable of being good parents and should not be denied this opportunity because of their disability. They do often require

President George H.W. Bush signs the Americans with Disabilities Act into law on July 26, 1990.

special help, or supports, which may or may not be available in a given community. Such supports can consist of in-home visits by a social worker to teach parenting skills; help with shopping, money management, and health care; help with transportation of the family; and links to parenting groups to help teach and reinforce parenting skills.

The California-based group called Through the Looking Glass has been providing support to intellectually disabled parents since the 1980s. They provide information, consultation, materials, and training nationwide to many such parents and have successfully kept many families with mentally retarded parents together. They also help establish support groups to help these parents learn parenting skills from other parents and have reported a great deal of success with these endeavors. One of the mothers involved in a local support group wrote:

> I really love the mothers group. It really helps me a lot, my son likes it very much. He loves the animals, and the teaching, friends. Sometimes when things are hard, I share with the group and it makes me feel better. I really think we should continue, the moms group, its very important to us. The group helps me be more patient to my son. It makes me proud to be a mom. Sometimes I talk about my son being frustrated, and upset. I share it with the group, and it makes me feel not alone, because the other mothers are going through the same thing. Thank you.[18]

A Diversity of Capabilities

The challenges faced by parents with mental retardation illustrates the diverse range of capabilities and life situations of the intellectually disabled. Depending on the degree of mental and physical disability, some individuals are capable of social interactions, dating, and marriage, while others are not. Experts say it is important for parents of the mentally retarded individual to recognize early on whether such relationships are possible and, if so, to instruct the child on how to behave socially. Acceptable speech and behavior must be taught to prevent embarrassment and harm to others, as many mentally retarded persons are unaware of how to act around peers and people of other ages. Self-protection should also be taught so the person will be safe from those who may seek to harm him or her. One area that experts say is very important to teach mentally retarded people is how to protect themselves from sexual abuse, which is quite common in this population.

Those who have mental retardation but who are capable of marriage generally marry others who also suffer from mental retardation. But those who are capable of having friends often want to be friends with nondisabled people so as to be more included in society and to validate their self-worth as a person.

It is not always easy for them to make friends, but it is nonetheless important. As Troy, a teen with Down syndrome, said in a speech to his class when he graduated from high school:

I am a person with disabilities and when I say "my friends" I mean friends, real friends just like everyone else, I have

A mentally retarded couple. Most people who have mental retardation generally marry others with MR.

friends. Most of you think all people have friends, but for people with disabilities friends are not always real. . . . The law says that I can come to school, but no law can make me have friends. But then some kids started to think that I was okay, first it was just one or two kids who were nice to me. They found out that I cared about them and I loved my school. I told them I want to have real friends. Others started to hang out with me, and they found out we could be friends. We started to learn together that in some ways we were different but in some ways we were the same. They called me friend and made sure that I was in everything at school . . . the law says that I am included, but it is my friends who say . . . "TD [Troy's nickname], come sit by me."[19]

Troy received a standing ovation for his speech, and news of his final words, "come sit by me," spread throughout the world. In Australia the Special Olympics Program, which is a worldwide program that allows people with mental retardation to receive training and compete with other similar athletes in Olympic-type events, adopted those words as a motto for in-

Community of Caring

Even when mentally retarded children attend mainstream schools and classrooms, they have difficulties making friends and being accepted by their nondisabled peers. The Community of Caring organization was founded in 1982 by Eunice Kennedy Shriver to address issues like these as well as to provide education to reduce preventable forms of mental retardation. Community of Caring staff members provide workshops for teachers and students that teach them about the needs and contributions of mentally retarded children. Research has shown that these workshops have significantly resulted in more positive views toward disabled students and in more positive school and social experiences for these children.

clusion and made pins bearing the slogan. Athletes from Australia who attended the 2003 Special Olympics World Summer Games in Dublin, Ireland, brought pins to give to their fellow athletes from around the world.

Special Olympics

Over 1.7 million people in over 150 countries compete in Special Olympics, and research shows that the benefits of this participation are immense. Athletes, coaches, and families report improvements in self-image, social skills, and overall health. In addition, over half of the adults in Special Olympics have regular jobs, compared with about 10 percent of the mentally retarded people who do not participate in Special Olympics.

Andy, who has Down syndrome, talked about how participation in swimming and later in Special Olympics helped him not only physically, but also led to him becoming a Special Olympics coach, a Swimming USA coach and junior lifeguard, and a spokesperson for The Arc of South Florida:

I was born with no physical problems, my heart was fine and everything else that could have gone wrong didn't. The problems I had went along with having Downs. I had very low tone in all my muscles, so it made it very hard to sit, crawl, and of course, walk. All through my early months I had intense physical therapy and in spite of it, I still wasn't making the progress that my mom wanted to see. . . . The doctors told my mom that regardless of the fact that I had Downs, I still carried my family's genes. Whatever we had excelled in life, I should benefit from. Having come from a family of swimmers, in the water I went at the early age of nine months. To my doctor's amazement, in three months of swimming I could swim like a frog underwater and even hold my head up. My lack of muscle tone was quickly disappearing. Though they had predicted I wouldn't walk until age two or three, I made liars of them all and started walking at 13 months. Swimming turned me into someone who beat all the odds and still today I continued through swimming to succeed.[20]

Children running in the fifty-meter race at the Special Olympics in Enid, Oklahoma.

Other disabled athletes find similar success and enrichment of their lives. Jen, for example, from Portland, Oregon, won a bronze medal in track and also competed in alpine skiing, basketball, football, softball, roller-skating, tennis, swimming, and gymnastics at Special Olympics. She earned a varsity letter in track and field at her high school and was the only girl at the school to pass the U.S. Marine Corps physical testing.

Eduardo of Guatemala also used Special Olympics as a springboard for competing with nondisabled athletes. He first entered local and international Special Olympics in swimming, running, and cycling and won many medals. He began competing in triathlons throughout the world, including eleven Ironman Triathlons, and gained international recognition for his achievements. He excelled and finished ahead of many nondisabled athletes and, among other awards, received the Sportsman of the Year award in 1996 in Guatemala, the silver cup in the VI Dualthlon of San Juan de la Abadesa in Barcelona, Spain, and the Special Trophy of Ironman 1999 at the Lanzarote Triathlon.

Jobs and Living Arrangements

Athletics is not the only area in which some individuals with mental retardation find fulfillment and enrichment in life. Some are able to find jobs and live independently, while others remain dependent on parents, siblings, or other relatives or caretakers throughout their lives. Some live in special institutions, but the tendency is for them to live with relatives, in a group home, or by themselves.

Sometimes it is necessary to change these living arrangements if the person's capabilities change. People with Down syndrome, for example, who are over age forty have a higher-than-normal risk of getting Alzheimer's disease. One patient, Stephanie, had lived independently all her adult life when she suddenly lost her ability to feed herself, dress, toilet, and communicate and was moved to an Alzheimer's care center at age fifty-four. In a similar manner, Francis, aged sixty-eight, was placed in a nursing home when he became unable to work, neglected his appearance, and became incontinent, forgetful, angry, and argumentative.

Even those individuals who can live on their own as adults sometimes need a court-appointed guardian to look after their interests. For example, a person with mental retardation may not understand what is involved in purchasing a home or undergoing a medical procedure, and a guardian must be appointed to help them make the necessary decisions.

Some people who have mental disabilities are capable of what is known as competitive employment—that is, they have skills equivalent to those of workers without disabilities and

Some mentally retarded people are able to find jobs and live independently. This man has been working at the Sheraton hotel for twenty years.

can hold a job on their own. Troy, who has Down syndrome, is able to work as a cashier at a convenience store and is a team manager for the football, hockey, and baseball teams at the local high school. He does not require special job coaching. Other retarded people may require supported employment, where a job coach assists them with understanding and performing a job. Still others are able to work in a sheltered workshop or work activity program that is designed specifically for those with disabilities and involves full-time supervision by nondisabled people.

Still, most mentally retarded people are unemployed for a variety of reasons. These include the fact that many who have mental retardation do not receive vocational training while in school, even though it is officially required under IDEA. Also, many do not know how to go about obtaining employment, and many employers are hesitant to hire someone who has mental retardation because of preconceived notions that the person is incapable of doing a good job.

Studies have shown, however, that once they are trained to do a job, most mentally retarded people are as competent and dependable as are nondisabled workers. Among the jobs where workers with retardation have proven to be competitive are animal caretakers, laundry workers, building maintenance workers, library assistants, data entry clerks, factory workers, radio and television repair technicians, nursing aides, and housekeepers.

Rarely, individuals with mental retardation are able to run their own businesses. One example reported in an issue of The Arc's newsletter involved Greg Prater, a thirty-five-year-old mentally retarded man in Maryland who started his own vending machine business with assistance from The Arc, the state's Division of Rehabilitation Services, and the Reach Independence Through Self-Employment Program. Once he obtained the needed financing, Prater launched the business and continues to see a healthy increase in profits. It is unusual, however, for a mentally retarded person to have the skills and knowledge necessary to run a business.

Challenges for the Family

Not only does living with mental retardation offer special challenges for the mentally retarded person, but it also can be difficult for the families of the mentally disabled, especially when the impairment is severe. Parents of such individuals must often attend to the person's needs round the clock. Sometimes the federal and state governments offer monetary assistance and respite care to families who care for a disabled person at home, but even with such assistance the challenges are still there. Many parents report an ongoing sense of grief and frustration in knowing that their child will never achieve a totally "normal" life. Some families join support groups so they can interact with and share stories and helpful tips with others who are going through the same thing. These groups may be local, national, or even international. Some have actual meetings, while others are accessed via the Internet.

Recently, advocacy organizations for the mentally retarded have realized that brothers and sisters of those with mental retardation face unique challenges in growing up. These organizations have begun special outreach programs for siblings to allow them to share and grow from their experiences. Many siblings feel guilty that they themselves are not disabled. Some are embarrassed about the brother or sister who is disabled and do not invite friends over for this reason. Others are jealous over the amount of attention the mentally retarded sibling receives or may feel like they have to excel at everything to make up for the disabled child.

Positive Effects on Siblings
However, studies show that being the sibling of a disabled person can also have positive effects. According to The Arc:

> Researchers have found that children in families where a sibling has a disability can become more mature, responsible, self-confident, independent and patient. These siblings can also become more altruistic (charitable), more sensitive to humanitarian efforts and have a greater sense of closeness to family. Growing up with a sibling who has a disability may instill a greater level of understanding and development in the siblings who are not disabled. They may develop greater leadership skills, especially in areas where understanding and sensitivity to human awareness issues are important.[21]

Austin, whose sister Ashley has mental disabilities, became a stronger, more compassionate, and more tolerant person as a result of growing up with a disabled sibling. As he wrote in an article for *Insight:*

When I was about 6 or 7, I rode the bus to school every day. All the kids on the bus were from my neighborhood and they all knew Ashley. But on that bus, I remember that the kids would use the fact that my sister had mental retardation against us like it was something bad. They would say things like, "At least I don't have a retarded sister," as if I have a disease or that I was not like them because of it. From this experience, I have learned to block out what others say about people who are different. I have learned not to accept the word "retarded." I think that every day, I hear someone use that word. From my experience, knowing someone that is different from you is a great thing and you can learn a lot.[22]

Raising a mentally retarded child can be difficult for families, especially if the child's impairment is severe.

Life Is Better than Ever

Despite the fact that living with mental retardation is challenging for affected persons and their families, most agree that life today with the condition is better than it was in the past, when most individuals who suffered with mental retardation were hidden away in institutions or at home without entering the mainstream of society. And as advocates strive for even more inclusion and as research is conducted to help make life with mental retardation easier, the future for mentally disabled people looks brighter.

CHAPTER FIVE

The Future

Although people with mental retardation have come a long way over the past several decades in being integrated into society and in having certain legal rights, advocates say there is still much to do before their goals are realized. As stated in The Arc's position statement, these goals include the notions that

> our constituents have the same right to self-determination as all people and must have the freedom, authority, and support to exercise control over their lives. . . . All our constituents have the right to participate fully in their diverse communities. Needed supports should be available and affordable so that each individual with disabilities can live, learn, work, and play with others who do not have disabilities.[23]

In order to achieve these goals, advocacy organizations and individuals alike are active in educating the public, educators, and government officials about the needs and capabilities of people with mental disabilities. They lobby lawmakers so that laws favorable to their cause will be passed. They teach parents of disabled children how to make sure their children have access to school and social activities as much as possible. They educate disabled adults about their rights, responsibilities, and capacity to make a difference by voting and writing to government officials if they are able to do so.

Health-Care Needs for the Future

One area in which advocates are lobbying for support is the area of health care. People who have mental retardation are living longer than they used to, and this means that government support for their health care must last longer. Many people do not receive adequate health care either, and the AAMR and other groups are trying to get the government and health-care providers to improve access to health care. Authorities have taken these efforts to heart, and the U.S. surgeon general issued a report outlining future goals that include:

1. Integrate health promotion into community environments of people with mental retardation.
2. Increase knowledge and understanding of health and mental retardation, ensuring that knowledge is made practical and easy to use.
3. Improve the quality of health care for people with mental retardation.
4. Train health care providers in the care of adults and children with mental retardation.
5. Ensure that health care financing produces good health outcomes for adults and children with mental retardation.
6. Increase sources of health care services for adults, adolescents, and children with mental retardation, ensuring that health care is easily accessible for them.[24]

Other organizations are also striving to improve health-care services for people who suffer from mental retardation. For example, the American Academy of Family Physicians and Special Olympics have formed a partnership that seeks to improve access to health care and to healthy physical activity. Currently, only about one in fifty primary care physicians have a minimum of training to treat people with mental retardation. Special Olympics plans to develop an online database of physicians willing to treat patients with intellectual disabilities. In addition, the partnership will establish educational courses for physicians and create curricula in medical schools that teach doctors and aspiring doctors how to care for people with mental retardation.

Criminal Justice

Another area in which advocates see a need for change and improvement is the arena of criminal justice. People with mental retardation are at higher-than-normal risk both for being victims and perpetrators of crimes. They are victims of crimes four to ten times as often as other people, and although they make up only about 2 percent of the population, they represent 4 to 10 percent of people in prison in the United States.

Experts at The Arc say that people with mental retardation become victims of crimes for several reasons. "Factors such as impaired cognitive abilities and judgement, physical disabilities, insufficient adaptive behaviors, constant interactions with 'protectors' who exploit them, lack of knowledge on how to protect themselves and living and working in high-risk environments increase the vulnerability to victimization."[25] When people with mental retardation are the victims of crime, they may not know how to report it. If they do report it, law enforcement personnel may not take them seriously, and the mentally disabled person may not know how to get a lawyer to prosecute.

Crimes committed by mentally disabled people range from theft to assault and murder. Often the person is used by another criminal to commit an act that he or she does not understand is wrong. Some people have a strong need to be accepted and will help with criminal activities to gain acceptance. In the case of Billy Dwayne White, a teenager with mental retardation, the boy committed crimes encouraged by older men in his neighborhood. One of these men testified:

> When Billy started hanging around us he was real scared and timid. We told him that he would have to change. We taught him how to steal. We would get him to do things that were wrong by telling him that he was a coward if he didn't, and that he could only be in our gang if he showed us that he had courage. . . . We could persuade him to do these things because he was easily misled.[26]

Once confronted by police, people who have mental retardation will often say what they think the police want to hear

Daryl Renard Atkins, who tested with an IQ of 59, was convicted of murder and given the death sentence. In 2002 the U.S. Supreme Court ruled that mentally disabled people could not be executed for their crimes.

and thus end up being convicted of crimes even if they are not guilty. One well-known example of a situation where a mentally retarded man was unjustly convicted of committing a crime occurred in Aurora, Missouri, in 1986. Twenty-year-old Johnny Lee Wilson was arrested for the murder of seventy-nine-year-old Pauline Martz and signed a confession saying he committed the crime even though he had not done so and there was no evidence against him. At a court hearing Wilson accepted a plea bargain and went to prison. Nine years later the governor of Missouri pardoned him because defense attorneys produced evidence that Wilson had been forced into signing the confession without understanding what he was doing, even though he was actually innocent. Advocates for the disabled say this type of thing happens fairly frequently and that those with mental retardation need to have legal protections to prevent wrongful convictions.

Cruel and Unusual Punishment

One area where legal protections have been established is in relation to capital punishment. It used to be that mentally disabled people convicted of a capital crime could be executed, but in 2002 the U.S. Supreme Court ruled that this constituted cruel and unusual punishment because people who have mental retardation are not competent to understand what they have done. The case that led to this decision was the Daryl Renard Atkins case. Atkins, aged twenty-seven, had an IQ of 59 and had never lived on his own or held a job. He was scheduled to be executed in Virginia, where he was convicted of shooting a man for beer money in 1996. In explaining its reasons for the ruling, the Court wrote, "We are not persuaded that the execution of mentally retarded criminals will measurably advance the deterrent or the retributive purpose of the death penalty."[27]

Even though those who have mental retardation can no longer be executed for killing someone, advocates say there is still a long way to go before they are treated fairly in the criminal justice system. An article on The Arc Web site says:

Education and training is vital if individuals with intellectual disabilities are going to receive equal justice. Children, adolescents, and adults with this disability must learn about the possibility of meeting a police officer, how to protect their rights during encounters with police and how to speak up if they are being victimized. Cross-training needs to occur among all professionals in schools, police departments, victim assistance agencies and in the courtroom as a way to start opening the lines of communication between these systems. In the schools, concerned parents can contact their school's special education department

and request the use of such training if it is currently un-
available. They can also contact their local police department and ask for the training officer or police chief as well
as the victim assistance department. . . . Educating court officials can begin by contacting the court liaison and re-
questing a meeting with the judge to see what training is
currently provided. Building these alliances can prepare
the community for situations involving people with intellectual disabilities who come in contact with the criminal
justice system either as victims or suspects.[28]

Medical Research

Besides promoting advocacy to improve the lives of those who
suffer from mental retardation, a plethora of organizations are
involved in research to make life easier and perhaps prevent
or even cure certain types of mental retardation. Much of this
research is conducted at fourteen Mental Retardation Developmental Disabilities Research Centers throughout the United
States and at other research centers throughout the world.

Gene Therapy and Genetic Research

At one of the centers, the Center on Human Development and
Disability in Seattle, Washington, for example, investigators
are conducting studies seeking to identify genes associated
with mental retardation and to develop methods of replacing
defective genes through gene therapy. There are currently four
approaches to gene therapy. The most common is to insert a
normal gene into the body's genetic material. The second
method involves removing an abnormal gene and replacing it
with a normal gene using a process known as homologous re-
combination. The third method is to repair an abnormal gene
through a process called selective reverse mutation, and the
fourth involves regulating a specific gene to enhance or dimin-
ish its level of activity. All of these methods are in the experimental stages and may someday prove to be useful in treating
mental retardation that is caused by a specific gene. Investigators are studying whether it is possible to replace faulty genes
before a baby is born as well as trying to do this after birth.

As scientists come closer to making gene therapy successful, ethical questions as to its desirability and appropriateness arise. The authors of *Understanding Mental Retardation* discuss the ethics of these procedures:

As genetic research continues its rapid advance, society must define normality and disability while being cautious about who makes the determination. We must decide whether normality for all is a desired outcome or if genetic

A geneticist examines the arrangement of a patient's chromosomes.

diversity is more desirable. . . . As human genome research allows us to read the blueprint for each individual, there will be a temptation to pre-select "desirable" traits in the formation of human embryos and to "deselect" undesirable embryos. Many people argue that this will bring an end to tragic hereditary disabilities. It also may reintroduce the specter of eugenics."[29]

Eugenics is the science of improving the genetic composition of humans. Adolf Hitler used the idea of eugenics to try to "cleanse" Europe of what he deemed to be inferior groups of people, such as the mentally retarded, in the 1930s and 1940s. Some experts worry that trying to build "ideal" human beings through gene therapy would lead to similar bigotry and discrimination.

Persistent Researchers

At another research center, the University of Pennsylvania School of Medicine in Philadelphia, one area of investigation focuses on how different cognitive impairments seen in different forms of mental retardation are related to variations in brain structure. According to The Arc: "This research may help to identify specific regions of the brain as origins for different aspects of thought processes. They may also lead to innovative approaches to educational programming that could be specified to certain cognitive defects."[30]

One important project at the John F. Kennedy Center for Research on Education and Human Development at Vanderbilt University in Nashville, Tennessee, is studying the genetics of Prader-Willi syndrome. Researchers are trying to develop methods of preventing the syndrome, which is caused by an abnormality on chromosome 15, by finding out which gene or genes are involved and exactly how these genes regulate body chemistry and behavior.

Other researchers are looking for genes that cause different types of mental retardation. In one 2004 study at Beth Israel Deaconess Medical Center in Boston, Massachusetts, scientists identified the gene responsible for a newly recognized type of mental retardation known as bilateral frontoparietal polymicrogyria (BFPP). It is caused by the gene GPR56 located on chromosome 16. BFPP is characterized by mental retardation, walking difficulty, language impairment, and seizures. The gene disorder that causes BFPP results in abnormal shape and size of the brain's frontal lobes, the part of the brain that controls social function, cognition, language, and problem solving.

Extensive work on mental retardation is also underway at the Shriver Mental Retardation Center in Waltham, Massachusetts,

Bilateral Frontal Polymicrogyria

A laboratory at Beth Israel Deaconess Medical Center in Massachusetts is studying a newly discovered cause of mental retardation called bilateral frontal polymicrogyria. They describe it as

a newly recognized genetic disorder with autosomal recessive inheritance. This means that most children with this disorder are born to parents who are "silent carriers" of a mutation that may never have presented itself in the family before. Usually, our brains have folds in the cortex (the outer layer) that increase the surface area of our brains. These folds are referred to as gyri. When an individual has polymicrogyria, there are many more folds than usual but each fold is very small. With BFPP, the polymicrogyria is primarily found in the front and the parietal lobes of the brain. The diagnosis is made by brain imaging with a CT scan or MRI (magnetic resonance imaging). Individuals with BFPP often have moderate mental retardation and seizures, with the onset of seizures frequently after 3 years of age. Many individuals with BFPP also have esotropia (crossed eyes).

Beth Israel Deaconess Medical Center, "Bilateral Frontal Polymicrogyria." www.bidmc.harvard.edu/display.asp?leaf_id=5858.

named for Eunice Kennedy Shriver, a woman who has done much to help people with mental retardation. One important project at this center involves genes that seem to be related to the nerve damage seen in aging people with Down syndrome and with Alzheimer's disease. Investigators are studying how the tau gene malfunctions to cause damage to the axons of nerve cells. An axon is the part of the nerve cell that transmits information in the form of chemical messengers and electrical impulses to other nerve cells. By delineating the functions of this gene, the researchers hope to manipulate it to prevent the damage it does.

Eunice Kennedy Shriver

Eunice Kennedy Shriver has been a leader for several decades in the campaign to improve the lives of people who suffer with mental retardation. Born in 1921 in Brookline, Massachusetts, to Joseph P. and Rose Kennedy, Shriver is the sister of former U.S. president John F. Kennedy. Her sister Rosemary, who had mental retardation, inspired Shriver and her family to work tirelessly for the betterment of the intellectually disabled worldwide.

In 1957 Shriver took over the direction of the Joseph P. Kennedy Jr. Foundation, an organization founded in 1946 as a memorial to her brother Joseph P. Kennedy Jr., who was killed in World War II. The foundation's goals are to identify the causes of mental retardation, to prevent the disorder from occurring, and to improve the way society treats people who have the disorder. Under Shriver's leadership, many advances have been made, including the establishment of the President Kennedy Committee on Mental Retardation in 1961, the development of the National Institute for Child Health and Human Development in 1962, and the establishment of a network of mental retardation research centers at major medical schools across the United States. In 1968 Shriver also founded the Special Olympics and remains honorary chairperson of this organization.

Another type of genetic research involves studying members of families where one or more people have a particular disease or condition in order to discover patterns of inheritance and to localize and identify specific genes. An additional type of genetic study is aimed at developing genetic tests for certain conditions. These tests may include screening tests for newborns, carrier status tests to determine if certain individuals carry a gene or chromosome abnormality that may affect future offspring, prenatal tests for mutations, and risk assessment tests to determine the probability that an individual will develop a genetically linked disease in the future.

Such research can help individuals and families in dealing with a genetic disorder or in planning whether or not to have children because of the presence of certain genetic mutations in the parents. It can also have adverse effects, such as being psychologically disturbing to affected individuals and family members who discover undesirable facts about their genetics. It can be detrimental, too, if medical insurers or prospective employers find out the results of genetic tests, because such entities are known to discriminate against people with genetic disorders. This is why researchers are careful to obtain the informed consent of people who participate in these sorts of research studies. By law, the investigators are required to make the nature and risks of the research understandable to all participants. If the participant is a child or is incapable of understanding what is involved, a parent or guardian is allowed to make the decision for him or her.

Biochemistry and Drugs

Two additional areas of current and future research involve biochemistry and drugs. In one recent study at the University of Florida in Gainesville, investigators found a biochemical explanation for how PKU causes mental retardation. People born with PKU are deficient in an enzyme that converts the amino acid phenylalanine into a usable form. The phenylalanine builds up to toxic levels in the blood, resulting in brain disorders such as mental retardation. Prior to this research, no one knew how the buildup of this chemical led to brain disorders.

But the researchers found that high levels of phenylalanine interfere with the neurotransmitter glutamate, a chemical messenger that plays a key role in brain development and function. An article in *UF News* explains: "The process is akin to a baseball game gone bad. Imagine if a pitcher were joined by six players simultaneously winding up on the mound. Crouched behind home plate, the single catcher would soon be overwhelmed. Even if the coach sent in teammates to catch the extra balls, confusion would reign on the field."[31]

A Promising Drug

Doctors are also researching medications that might improve the mental faculties of people with mental retardation. Recent investigations at the Duke University Medical Center in Durham, North Carolina, focused on a drug approved to treat Alzheimer's disease that also seems to improve attention span, communication, and mood in children with Down syndrome. The drug is called donepezil hydrochloride, brand named Aricept®. Alzheimer's disease results at least partly from a failure of the brain to produce enough acetylcholine. Aricept® works by blocking an enzyme that normally breaks down the neurotransmitter acetylcholine in the brain. The brains of people with Down syndrome also fail to produce enough of this chemical messenger, so the researchers reasoned that giving Down syndrome patients Aricept® might improve their mental faculties.

The effectiveness of Aricept® was measured through a series of standardized language tests that assessed the ability to interpret pictures, repeat sentences of increasing complexity, and make associations among related words. The investigators reported that the children given Aricept® showed dramatic improvements in these skills over the course of the study. The parents of these children also reported that the children were more expressive than usual about likes and dislikes, better able to make everyday connections, and were more easily engaged in conversation. The researchers are optimistic that, if future studies prove the drug to be truly effective, this could be of significant help to people with Down syndrome. "A therapy that could change the lives of people with Down syndrome

Researchers at the Duke University Medical Center have been studying the effect of Aricept® on people with Down syndrome.

early in childhood, making them more active learners, could really maximize their benefit and quality of life,"[32] said researcher Priya Kishnani.

The Road Ahead

The ultimate goal of all this research and advocacy is to make the lives of those with mental retardation easier and more fulfilling in the future. While acknowledging that much progress has been made, the authors of National Goals and Research for People with Intellectual and Developmental Disabilities point out that there is still much to do before these goals are achieved:

More than 100,000 people with intellectual and developmental disabilities remain institutionalized in the United States. Many others, while not institutionalized according to common definitions, have little control over where, with whom, and how they live in their communities. Large numbers of these people want opportunities to contribute to their communities through useful part-time employment. Tens of thousands of individuals and families have no access to basic services that would offer, at the least, a modicum of control over their lives.[33]

Those who have not yet achieved inclusion and self-determination, however, have powerful organizations and researchers on their side, and the fight ahead looks more hopeful than it ever did in the past.

Notes

Introduction: What's in a Name?
1. Quoted in Kathy Smallwood, "Troy Daniels," Special Olympics. www.specialolympics.org/Special+Olympics +Public+Website/English/Compete/Meet_our_Athletes/ Daniels%2c+Troy. htm.
2. Quoted in Stephen R. Schroeder et al., "Usage of the Term 'Mental Retardation': Language, Image, and Public Education," Social Security Online. www.ssa.gov/disability /MentalRetardationReport.pdf.
3. The Arc, "Self-Determination." www.thearc.org/posits/self detpos.htm.

Chapter 1: What Is Mental Retardation?
4. Quoted in Patricia Ainsworth and Pamela C. Baker, *Understanding Mental Retardation*. Jackson: University Press of Mississippi, 2004, p. 66.
5. Quoted in Ainsworth and Baker, *Understanding Mental Retardation*, p. 68.
6. Fran Davidson, "Parent's Pride," National Fragile X Foundation. www.fragilex.org/NewsletrWinter2004.pdf.
7. Quoted in Angelman Syndrome Foundation, "Facts About Angelman Syndrome." www.angelman.org/angel/index. php?id=75.

Chapter 2: What Causes Mental Retardation?
8. American Association on Mental Retardation, "Windows of Vulnerability: An Overview of Brain Development and Susceptibility to Environmental Contaminants." www.aamr.org/ToxinsandMentalRetardation/pdf/Web_ Paper_4_Schettler.pdf.

9. Ainsworth and Baker, *Understanding Mental Retardation*, p. 13.

10. Ainsworth and Baker, *Understanding Mental Retardation*, p. 32.

11. Human Rights Watch, "Mental Retardation: An Overview." www.hrw.org/reports/2001/ustat/ustat0301-01.htm.

Chapter 3: Prevention, Remediation, and Treatment

12. U.S. Department of Health and Human Services, "U.S. Surgeon General Releases Advisory on Alcohol Use in Pregnancy." www.hhs.gov/surgeongeneral/pressreleases/sg02222005.html.

13. The Arc, "The Individuals with Disabilities Act (IDEA): Eligibility, IEP's, and Placement." www.thearc.org/faqs/qa-idea.html.

14. The Arc, "The Moral Imperative of Inclusion." www.thearc.org/insight/2005a/16.pdf.

15. The Arc, "Aging, Mental Retardation, and Physical Fitness." www.thearc.org/faqs/fitnessage.html.

Chapter 4: Living with Mental Retardation

16. Quoted in The Arc, "Membership in America." www.thearc.org/insight/2004b/page4.pdf.

17. The Arc, "Parents with Intellectual Disabilities." www.thearc.org/faqs/parentswithid.doc.

18. Quoted in Sherrie Hansen and Megan Kirshbaum, "TLG's Intervention Model and New Training Module Concerning Parents with Intellectual Disabilities," *Through the Looking Glass*, Fall 2005.

19. Quoted in Smallwood, "Troy Daniels."

20. Quoted in Special Olympics, "Andres 'Andy' Miyares." www.specialolympics.org/Special+Olympics+Public+Web site/English/Compete/Meet_our_Athletes/Miyares%2c+Andres.htm.

21. The Arc, "Siblings: Brothers and Sisters of People Who Have Mental Retardation." www.thearc.org/faqs/qa-siblings.html.

22. Austin Dolan, "My Experience," The Arc. www.thearc.org/insight//2003d2003issue.pdf.

Chapter 5: The Future

23. Quoted in The Arc, "Self-Determination and Full Inclusion." www.thearc.org/insight/2005a/02.pdf.

24. American Association on Mental Retardation, "Health Promotion for Persons with Intellectual and Developmental Disabilities." www.aamr.org/Reading_Room/pdf/HealthPromotionfm.pdf.

25. The Arc, "People with Intellectual Disabilities in the Criminal Justice System: Victims and Suspects." www.thearc.org/faqs/crimjustice.doc.

26. Quoted in Human Rights Watch, "Mental Retardation: An Overview." www.hrw.org/reports/2001/ustat/ustat 0301-01.htm.

27. Quoted in CNN.com, "Supreme Court Bars Executing Mentally Retarded." http://archives.cnn.com/2002/LAW/ 06/20/scotus.executions/ index.html.

28. The Arc, "People with Intellectual Disabilities in the Criminal Justice System."

29. Ainsworth and Baker, *Understanding Mental Retardation*, p. 164.

30. The Arc, "Mental Retardation and Developmental Disabilities Research Centers: An Overview of Current Genetic Research." www.thearc.org/pdf/gbr08.pdf.

31. *UF News*, "Cellular Communications Breakdown Identified in Inherited Brain Disorder." www.napa.ufl.edu/2005 news/pku.htm.

32. Quoted in *Duke Med News*, "Drug Might Boost Language Learning in Kids with Down Syndrome." www.dukemed news.org/news/article.php?id=8184.

33. K. Charlie Lakin and Ann P. Turnbull, eds., "National Goals and Research for People with Intellectual and Developmental Disabilities," AAMR Reading Room. www.aamr.org/Reading_Room?pdf/NationalGoalsfm.pdf.

Glossary

adaptive behaviors: The collection of concepts, social skills, and living skills that enable a person to function in everyday life.

chromosome: A wormlike body that houses genes in the nucleus of a cell.

developmental disability: A severe, chronic mental and/or physical impairment that begins before age twenty-two.

euthanasia: A procedure where a doctor kills an individual.

gene: The part of a DNA molecule that transmits hereditary information.

intelligence: General mental capability.

mental retardation: A condition involving brain disorders that lead to difficulty learning information and skills needed to adapt to the environment.

mutation: Damage to a gene or chromosome.

neurotoxic: Poisonous to the brain.

remediation: Special help or instruction.

sterilization: A surgical procedure that renders a person unable to reproduce.

Organizations to Contact

American Association on Mental Retardation (AAMR)
444 North Capitol St. NW, Suite 846
Washington, DC 20001-1512
(202) 387-1968 or (800) 424-3688
www.aamr.org

The AAMR promotes research, public policies, and advocacy
for individuals with mental retardation.

The Arc of the United States
1010 Wayne Ave., Suite 650
Silver Spring, MD 20910
(301) 565-3842
www.thearc.org

The Arc advocates and educates for the rights and full participation in society of the mentally retarded.

Centers for Disease Control and Prevention (CDC)
1600 Clifton Rd. NE
Atlanta, GA 30333
(404) 639-3534 or (800) 311-3435
www.cdc.gov

This Web site features comprehensive information about
mental retardation in its disabilities section.

National Information Center on Children and Youth with Disabilities
PO Box 1492
Washington, DC 20013
(800) 695-0285

www.nichcy.org

This Web site provides information on youth with disabilities,
including mental retardation.

For Further Reading

The Arc, "Community Living." www.thearc.org/faqs/comliv. html.

———, "The Individuals with Disabilities Act (IDEA): Eligibility, IEP's and Placement." www.thearc.org/faqs/qa-idea.html.

———, "Siblings: Brothers and Sisters of People Who Have Mental Retardation." www.thearc.org/faqs/qa-siblings.html.

Centers for Disease Control and Prevention, "Kid's Quest on Disability and Health." www.cdc.gov.ncbddd/kids/klalpage. htm.

Austin Dolan, "My Experience." www.thearc.org/insight//2003d/2003issued.pdf.

Laura Dolce, *Mental Retardation*. New York: Chelsea House, 1994. Discusses the history, characteristics, education, and treatment of mental retardation.

Leslie Johnson, "First—Do No Harm—an Argument Against Mandatory High-Stakes Testing for Students with Intellectual Disabilities." www.aamr.org/Reading_Room/pdf/MRAug 05highstakes.pdf.

KidsHealth, "Mental Retardation." www.kidshealth.org/kid/health_problems/birth_defect/mental_retardation.html.

Dawn M. Rudinski, "Buddy's Story," The Arc. www.thearc.org/insight/2004a/page6.pdf.

Index

Picture Credits

Cover photo: AP Images
AP Images, 22, 24, 43, 72, 82
Samuel Ashfield/Photo Researchers, Inc., 49
© Lester V. Bergman/CORBIS, 33
© Bettmann/CORBIS, 63
© Dennis Degnan/CORBIS, 52
John R. Foster/Photo Researchers, Inc., 39
© Tim Garcha/zefa/CORBIS, 69
Garo/Photo Researchers, Inc. Reproduced by permission, 38
The Granger Collection, New York, 54
© John Henley/CORBIS, 8
Kairos, Latin Stock/Photo Researchers, Inc., 34
James Keyser/Time Life Pictures/Getty Images, 44
© Rob Lewine/zefa/CORBIS, 15
© LWA-Dann Tardif/CORBIS, 77
© Tom and Dee Ann McCarthy/CORBIS, 85
© Mika/zefa/CORBIS, 20, 59
Phil Mislinski/Getty Images, 91
Temah Nelson. Reproduced by permission of Thomson Gale, 31
© Richard T. Nowitz/CORBIS, 17
© Steve Prezant/CORBIS, 48
© Ron Sachs/CNP/CORBIS, 67
© Ellen Senisi/The Image Works, 56
© Chris Ware/The Image Works, 74
© David H. Wells/CORBIS, 41
Steve Zmina, 21
© Jim Zuckerman/CORBIS, 30

About the Author

Melissa Abramovitz grew up in San Diego, California, and as a teenager developed an interest in medical topics. She began college with the intention of becoming a doctor but later switched majors, graduating summa cum laude from the University of California, San Diego, with a degree in psychology in 1976.

Launching her career as a writer in 1986 to allow herself to be an at-home mom when her two children were small, she realized she had found her niche. She continues to write regularly for magazines and educational book publishers and has published hundreds of articles and numerous short stories, poems, and books for children, teens, and adults. Many of her works are on medical topics.